INSIGHT ⊙ GUIDES

EXPLORE

FLORENCE

PLAN & BOOK
YOUR TAILOR-MADE TRIP

 BRAZIL
 CHILE
 ECUADOR

TAILOR-MADE TRIPS & UNIQUE EXPERIENCES CREATED BY LOCAL TRAVEL EXPERTS AT INSIGHTGUIDES.COM/HOLIDAYS

Insight Guides has been inspiring travellers with high-quality travel content for over 45 years. As well as our popular guidebooks, we now offer the opportunity to book tailor-made private trips completely personalised to your needs and interests.
By connecting with one of our local experts, you will directly benefit from their expertise and local know-how, helping you create memories that will last a lifetime.

HOW INSIGHTGUIDES.COM/HOLIDAYS WORKS

STEP 1

Pick your dream destination and submit an enquiry, or modify an existing itinerary if you prefer.

STEP 2

Fill in a short form, sharing details of your travel plans and preferences with a local expert.

STEP 3

Your local expert will create your personalised itinerary, which you can amend until you are completely satisfied.

STEP 4

Book securely online. Pack your bags and enjoy your holiday! Your local expert will be available to answer questions during your trip.

BENEFITS OF PLANNING & BOOKING AT INSIGHTGUIDES.COM/HOLIDAYS

PLANNED BY LOCAL EXPERTS
The Insight Guides local experts are hand-picked, based on their experience in the travel industry and their impeccable standards of customer service.

SAVE TIME & MONEY
When a local expert plans your trip, you save time and money when you book, even during high season. You won't be charged for using a credit card either.

TAILOR-MADE TRIPS
Book with Insight Guides, and you will be in complete control of the planning process, from the initial selections to amending your final itinerary.

BOOK & TRAVEL STRESS-FREE
Enjoy stress-free travel when you use the Insight Guides secure online booking platform. All bookings come with a money-back guarantee.

WHAT OTHER TRAVELLERS THINK ABOUT TRIPS BOOKED AT INSIGHTGUIDES.COM/HOLIDAYS

Trip to Portugal

Every step of the planning process and the trip itself was effortless and exceptional. Our special interests, preferences and requests were accommodated resulting in a trip that exceeded our expectations.

Corinne, USA   ★★★★★

Trip to Vietnam

The organization was superb, the drivers professional, and accommodation quite comfortable. I was well taken care of! My thanks to your colleagues who helped make my trip to Vietnam such a great experience.

Heather   ★★★★★

DON'T MISS OUT
BOOK NOW AT
INSIGHTGUIDES.COM/HOLIDAYS

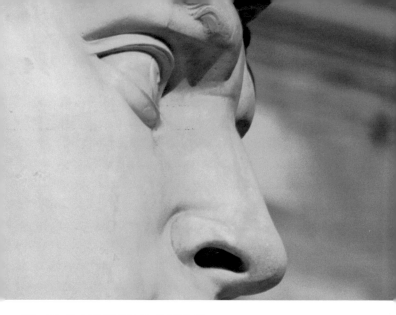

CONTENTS

Introduction

Directory

Credits

Best Routes

ART ENTHUSIASTS

Don't miss the Uffizi Gallery, the world's best collection of Renaissance art (route 3), or the Accademia (route 6), home to Michelangelo's *David*. Walk 4 covers the Bargello's sculpture and the famed Santa Croce frescoes.

RECOMMENDED ROUTES FOR...

CHILDREN

Keep kids amused in the Boboli Garden (route 9), the Children's Museum (route 2) or the Archaeological Museum (route 6), which has mummies. Then treat them to ice cream at Vivoli (route 4).

FOOD AND WINE

Good routes for foodies include no. 5, which heads to the Mercato Centrale with its food stalls and cafés. Route 7 ends at one of the city's most popular tripe stands – not for the faint-hearted, but certainly authentic.

MEDICI FLORENCE

Route 2 visits the Palazzo Vecchio, erstwhile home of the Medici, while their family tombs are in the Medici Chapels (route 5). Route 12 takes you out of the city centre to focus on several villas built for the Medici.

PARKS AND GARDENS

The city's main park, the Boboli Garden (route 9), showcases statuary, grottoes and formal gardens, as well as the Pitti Palace. The Medici Villas (route 12) are also notable for their lovely gardens.

RIVAL CITIES

Easy day trips from Florence include long-time rivals Siena (route 14), Pisa (route 15) and San Gimignano (route 13) – a superb hilltop village and the best-preserved medieval settlement in the country.

SHOPPING

Pop into the Mercato Centrale on route 5 for local shopping (especially food). Alternatively, take a stroll along Via de' Tornabuoni, the city's most prestigious shopping street, and then end at the Mercato Nuovo, on route 7.

VIEWS

The best views are from Piazzale Michelangelo and San Miniato al Monte church (route 10). The Boboli Garden (route 9) is also a great lookout. For splendid Tuscan countryside, head to Fiesole (route 11).

INTRODUCTION

An introduction to Florence's geography, customs and culture, plus illuminating background information on cuisine, history and what to do when you're there.

The view from Piazzale Michelangelo

EXPLORE FLORENCE

Famous for its contributions to science, literature, art and architecture, the city state of Florence is where the modern world began, and today it still retains a lively mix of dissent and luxury, the sublime and the earthy.

In most people's minds the name of Florence is indelibly linked to that of the Renaissance, when the extraordinarily rich flowering of artistic and intellectual life under the enlightened rule of the Medici, coupled with the city's immense banking wealth, made it the most important centre in Europe.

FLORENCE TODAY

Contemporary Florence is without doubt one of the finest open-air museums in the world, and the tourism that this fuels has itself become a major new source of wealth. Rarely, however, is it considered as a city in contemporary terms, except perhaps for its shopping. Yet even here, the fine handicrafts and stylish fashion accessories for which it is now almost equally famous are ultimately rooted in Florence's own early mercantile and creative traditions.

Yet struggling to break free of its historical straitjacket is another, more hidden Florence, which, when the surface is scratched, reveals itself to be a sophisticated, tuned-in, complex and even slightly troubled modern city, and anything but one suffering from the passive nature of a resigned tourist capital.

GEOGRAPHY AND LAYOUT

Built along the banks of the Arno, Florence is cut in two by the river, with the older part of the city lying to the north. The river has, perhaps, been a mixed blessing for the city – on the one hand supplying it with water and a transport link, but occa-

Picturesque Florentine rooftops

Historic street   *In the Boboli Garden*

sionally unleashing devastating floods, as happened in 1966 (see page 11).

Three squares

The old historic centre might be thought of as clustering around three *piazzi*, or squares, each of which represents a different centre of influence. Piazza del Duomo surrounds the city's cathedral and is the centre of spiritual power. To the north of here lie three of the city's major churches, Santa Maria Novella (close to the decidedly secular area around the railway station), San Lorenzo and San Marco.

To the south of Piazza del Duomo is Piazza della Signoria, surrounded by *palazzi* (palaces) with medieval crenellated towers. Here is the Palazzo Vecchio (Old Palace), from where the Medici ruled over Florence. It is still the centre of temporal power in the city, as home to the *Commune* (the city government).

To the west lies Piazza della Repubblica, the square laid out to represent a 'New Florence' during the 19th century, when the city was temporarily capital of the newly independent Italy. This might be seen as a symbol of the city's mercantile and artisan traditions. Close by are upmarket shopping streets and the main branches of the city's banks.

Across the Arno

The river not only provides a welcome sense of space after the narrow medieval streets of the old centre, it is also crossed by a number of elegant bridges, the most famous of which is the Ponte Vecchio. The views along the river are extremely beautiful, and the roads that run along its banks – popular for an evening stroll – are named after it: Lungarno (meaning 'Along the Arno').

Beyond the southern bank of the river is Oltrarno (Across the Arno), set-

The 1966 flood

On 4 November 1966, after 48cm (19in) of rain had fallen in 48 hours, the River Arno burst its banks. Thirty five people were killed, 16,000 vehicles destroyed and hundreds of homes left uninhabitable as the muddy floodwaters rose to more than 6m (20ft) above street level. Heating oil was swept out of broken basement tanks. The water crashed through the museums, galleries, churches and craft shops. Thousands of works of art were damaged. The city had suffered from floods in the past – about one really serious inundation each century – but this caused more damage than any other. Student volunteers flocked to Florence from around the world to help the army, which had sent in thousands of conscripts. Restorers estimated it would take 20 years for all the damaged art objects to be restored and for Florence to recover. They were half right. Florence has definitely recovered, and many works of art are back on display, but, almost half a century on, the task of restoration is still not yet complete.

Small is beautiful

tled later than the area to the north. This was for a long time a gritty working-class district, full of workshops, but is now becoming gentrified, with trendy bars (it is also popular with students), but still remains slightly off the main tourist routes. Dominating the area, however, is the grand palace of the Medici, the Palazzo Pitti, with the beautiful Boboli Garden beyond.

Overlooking it all, from its vantage point on top of the hills, is the shrine of Florence's first martyr, the glorious church of San Miniato al Monte.

A POTTED HISTORY

Beginnings
The first settlements in and around Florence were those of the peace-loving Etruscans (from whose name we get the modern Toscana, or Tuscany), who built a substantial town on the site of present-day Fiesole. They were to flourish until *c.*300 BC, when the region fell to the growing power of Rome. And it was the Romans who were to found the city of Firenze (Florence) in 59 BC, when they built a *colonia* for retired soldiers and named it Florentia.

The Commune
After the fall of Rome came the first glimmerings of the city-state, with the setting up of the *Commune*, and the construction of public works such as the city walls, a cathedral and the Palazzo Vecchio. However, it was with the rise of the wool trade, and then banking, from the 11th to the 13th centuries, that the city really began to assume its position of dominance.

By the 14th century Florence was the richest city in Europe, even though it often found itself at war with its neighbours, especially Siena – a rivalry that

Sleeping cat in Florence

Monk taking a break   *Mosaic of Christ in the Baptistry*

continues, albeit in a more gentle fashion, to the present day.

Renaissance flourishing

With its wealth, and numerous skilled artisans, Florence was the ideal candidate to be the city at the heart of the Renaissance. An extraordinary concentration of artistic talent, including Giotto, Masaccio, Uccello, Brunelleschi, Leonardo, Raphael and Michelangelo, to name but a few, found work and patronage in the city, especially once the Medici took control of Florence in 1434 (a period of rule that was to last, with a few breaks, until 1737).

Foreign rule

With the demise of the last of the Medici, Florence fell under foreign rule, first the Austrians and then the French. By this time, it was also being discovered by the British, who flocked to its art treasures

---

DON'T LEAVE FLORENCE WITHOUT...

Having breakfast Firenze-style. Start the day with a cappuccino and *cornetto* at Caffè Scudieri on the Piazza di San Giovanni (19r). This smart, long-established café/*pasticceria* is right in front of the Baptistry, in the pedestrianised Piazza. See page 35.

Climbing the Duomo. Amble around the Piazza, admiring the Baptistry, Campanile (bell tower) and the iconic Duomo (cathedral). Those with stamina can tackle the 463 stairs spiralling to the top of the cathedral's dome to admire Brunelleschi's engineering genius and the fabulous views. See page 29.

Shopping for Florentine leather. Florence is famed for its leather goods, which are typically of excellent quality and competitively priced; head to San Lorenzo market for leather bags, shoes and belts. If you're feeling flash, then go to Via de'Tornabuoni, home to the lavish flagship stores of Armani, Gucci and Prada, to name just a few. See page 54.

Eating tripe. Brave a tripe sandwich from the popular stands at the Mercato Centrale southwest corner. See page 67.

Admiring piazza art. Since medieval times the expansive Piazza della Signoria has been a hub of city life. Overlooking the piazza is the towering Palazzo Vecchio, former ancestral home of the Medici. Admire the array of open-air sculpture, check out the Gucci Museum, or sit at one of the people-watching cafés. See page 37.

Admiring the finest Renaissance art at the Uffizi. This repository of the world's finest collection of Renaissance art is a must-see, but book your tickets in advance unless you are happy to queue for a couple of hours. See page 44.

Taking in the view. The bastions of the Boboli Garden were designed by Michelangelo. The view, taking in the city and the Tuscan countryside beyond, is one of the most beautiful in Florence. Another sweeping view of the city centre is to be had from Piazzale Michelangelo and church of San Miniato. See pages 74 and 78.

as part of their 'grand tours' of the continent. Some of them came and expropriated works of art to hang in their stately homes, but others, captivated by the city, stayed and made it their home.

Unification and independence

When ideas of nationalism began to sweep through Europe during the 19th century, Tuscany was not immune, and became a major player in the *Risorgimento* (Revival) that ended with Italian unification and independence. Indeed, for five years, from 1865 to 1870, Florence was the capital of the new state. During this period, the city expanded rapidly; the city walls were demolished and replaced with a ring of avenues punctuated with large piazzas.

CONTEMPORARY FLORENCE

Since then Florence has survived Fascism under Mussolini, destruction under the Nazis, and dreadful flooding, but still remains one of the most beautiful cities in Europe with an artistic heritage unmatched almost anywhere. In many ways Florence has remained a prisoner of its original concept – namely, of a medieval Renaissance city – and finds it hard to move forward as a modern, progressive city. The sensation of being stuck in time is reinforced by the way foreign and Italian visitors, as well as Florentines, appear reluctant to consider the city in anything other than the most traditional terms. A good case in point is Japanese architect Arata Isozaki's design to build a towering, minimalist exit to the Uffizi Gallery, which has bitterly divided the city with critics dismissing it as a 'bus shelter'. The project is on ice and the stalemate has left the city hall, which sponsored the competition, in an embarrassing quandary.

MODERN MAYORS

Although the city might appear as though preserved in aspic, it is beginning to change. Thanks go first and foremost to Matteo Renzi, a young, forward-thinking man who rejuvenated the city's flagging politics when he was Florence's mayor in 2009–2014.

Bucking the trend of grey-haired politicians, the progressive and energetic Renzi became president of the Florentine province at 29, and mayor of Florence at

Florence's former mayor Matteo Renzi re-energised the city

View along the Arno

34 – the youngest to ever hold the post. He revitalised the city's cultural life, making museums more user-friendly, with longer opening hours and better ticketing. He also invested in eco-friendly transport to preserve the city's green spaces. No sooner was he elected mayor than he announced the surprise news that Piazza Duomo in the heart of the city would be banned to vehicles of any description, horses and carriages included. He accelerated the spread of high-speed internet and Wi-Fi in the city and posted his news on Twitter and Facebook.

Renzi went on to become Italy's prime minister in 2014, and he was replaced as Florence's mayor by Dario Nardella, another young and dynamic Democratic Party politician, who has worthily continued his predecessor's work. During his tenure the Uffizi's expansion and renovation has progressed, the Museo dell'Opera del Duomo was revamped and reopened in 2015 and the oldest theatre in Florence, the Teatro Niccolini, reopened in 2016 after a 20-year closure.

TOP TIPS FOR EXPLORING FLORENCE

Markets. Florence has many fascinating street markets, selling a variety of goods. For food head for the Mercato Centrale on Piazza del Mercato, or the Mercato di Sant' Ambrogio, Piazza Ghiberti. For leather goods try the Mercato Nuovo and, especially, the Mercato di San Lorenzo.

Entertainment listings. To keep up with the ever-changing scene, purchase *Firenze Spettacolo* (www.firenzespettacolo.it), the monthly listings magazine (with an English section) or the bi-weekly English magazine *The Florentine* (www.theflorentine.net); alternatively check the entertainment pages of *La Nazione*, the regional newspaper, or the Florence (Firenze) section of *La Repubblica*. The tourist information office at Via Cavour 1r (www.firenzeturismo.it) publishes a daily list of events.

Boboli concerts. Outside the main festival season, many concerts are held throughout the summer in cloisters, squares, churches and even in the Boboli Garden. Usually well advertised, these concerts may be of varying standard, but the settings are often highly evocative.

Vasari's home. Following several years of restoration the house where Vasari (1511–74) spent the last years of his life re-opened in 2012. The house has undergone many changes but the Sala Grande (Large Hall) remains intact, frescoed with works by Vasari and his contemporaries. The house can be visited by appointment (contact the Horne Museum, Via dei Benci 6, tel: 055-244 661).

Historic ball game. Piazza Santa Croce has been used as a football pitch since the 16th century. A plaque on the Palazzo dell'Antella at no. 21 marks the centre line of the pitch. *Calcio storico*, a rather violent early form of football, is still played here on the feast of San Giovanni (24 June).

Chef cooking with panache

FOOD AND DRINK

Tuscan food is often basic and frugal but extremely tasty, using the freshest vegetables and best cuts of meat. Helping to wash all this down are the wonderful local Chiantis, some of the finest of Italian wines.

Sobriety rather than sensuality is an important element in the Florentine character, and, despite their love of food, Florentines delight in simple and robust dishes, with plenty of vegetables and plainly grilled meats, nourishing and eaten for utility as much as enjoyment. Perhaps the reason for this lies in their history. As busy people in a thriving commercial environment, they had little time for over-sophistication, and this stolid element persists to this day. Thick soups and bean stews (served in terracotta pots whatever the restaurant) and large steaks and heavy wines are typical of a meal in Florence.

MARKETS AND VEGETABLES

Perhaps the best introduction to the city's food is a morning spent amid the vegetable stalls of the Mercato Centrale. Here, local produce – courgettes, tomatoes, mushrooms, peppers, potatoes and aubergines – of excellent quality can be seen piled high. Florentines will happily eat any of these vegetables fried or brushed with Tuscany's purest *Extra Vergine* olive oil, and simply grilled until soft and melting.

Fresh Tuscan vegetables are rarely disappointing on their own, but together they make two of the city's great specialities, *ribollita* and minestrone. *Ribollita* means 'reboiled', leftover vegetables; these are combined to create a dense soup, which might involve any spare vegetables but should traditionally include white *cannellini* beans and *cavolo nero*, a type of black cabbage indigenous to Tuscany. The soup is then thickened with stale bread.

Fagioli

But among these offerings, the undisputed aristocrats are the white beans or *fagioli*. Like the potato, the bean was introduced from the Americas by Florentine merchants, and it is now a staple of the city. In a soup or mixed with tuna fish, the little *fagioli* are a marvellously simple beginning to any Florentine meal. Best of all they are eaten plainly boiled with a dribbling of the new season's olive oil, thick, green and viscous, and utterly delicious.

Olive oil

Tuscany produces some of the world's finest olive oil, with the best of the Extra

Fresh anchovy starter

Serving up waffles

Virgin (*Extra Vergine*) ones having DOC (Denominazione D'Origine Controllata) status. From the region around Florence, look out for oils from Scansano, Seggiano and San Gimignano.

Chestnuts

These nuts – *castagne* in Italian – are a favourite in Tuscany, and from October onwards you will find them being roasted on the city's streets. Chestnuts are also made into flour and used to make pancakes, soups and sweet cakes.

MEAT DISHES

Although Florence can offer a cornucopia of vegetables, in practice it is meat that is held in highest regard. For a starter try *crostini di fegato*, chicken

Tuscan pizza

liver pâté on fried bread, delicious with a young white wine. Follow this with *fritto misto*, mixed meats fried in batter, or the peasant dish *stracotto*, beef stewed for several hours and especially satisfying in winter.

But, above all, Florence specialises in plain roasted and grilled meats: *arista* (roast pork), beef, lamb, especially at Easter, and even wild boar in season. Tuscany's fertile pasture produces some of the best meat in Italy, and the Florentines refuse to clutter these tastes with over-adornment. Just as simple is their treatment of chicken and pheasant.

However, the most prestigious of these – and as much a symbol of the city as the florin – is the famous *bistecca alla fiorentina* (steak Florentine). A huge, tender and succulent rib-steak from Tuscany's Chianina cattle, the *bistecca* is brushed with olive oil and charcoal-grilled over a scented wood fire of oak or olive branches, then seasoned with salt and pepper before being served, with a characteristic lack of fuss. It is simply the most delicious meat in Italy.

Another famous Florentine meat dish is *arista alla fiorentina*: roasted pork loin highly seasoned with chopped rosemary and ground pepper. The origin of this dish goes back to the 15th century. At the Ecumenical Council of 1430 in Florence, the Greek bishops were served the dish at a banquet and pronounced it *aristos*, which

Tuscan desserts are typically sophisticated

in Greek means 'very good'. The name stuck and became a feature of Florentine cuisine.

At the cheaper end of the culinary spectrum and in their rational desire not to waste, Florentines have even made a speciality out of tripe. *Trippa alla fiorentina*, cooked with tomatoes and sprinkled with parmesan, is a favourite and inexpensive dish.

SWEETS

If Florentine food tends to be filling, full of flavour and simple, Florentine *dolci* (desserts) make up for any lack of complexity. In the bars, cake shops and *gelaterie*, there is a riot of colour. *Coppe varie* – bowls of mixed fruit and water ice – compete for attention with pastries and handmade sweets, huge slabs

Chianti, the king of Florentine wines

of nougat, chocolate 'Florentines', *baci* (the angel's kiss) and, at carnival time, *schiacciata alla fiorentina*, a simple, light sponge cake.

One pride of the city is the incredibly rich, but delicious, *zuccotto*, a sponge-cake mould with a filling of almonds, hazelnuts, chocolate and cream. There is no general agreement, however, as to the origins of its name. Literally translated as 'small pumpkin', *zuccotto* – being a dome-shaped speciality – is thought by some to refer affectionately to the Duomo, or perhaps to be a slightly irreverent allusion to the clergy. In the Tuscan dialect, a cardinal's skull-cap is also called a *zuccotto*.

EATING OUT

As befits a city with so much excellent, hearty food, there are numerous places to eat. At the top end are the internationally renowned restaurants with Michelin stars, reinventing Tuscan classics for an eye-watering fee and a wine list that would break the bank at Monte Carlo.

These are, generally, for special occasions, but due to the straightforward nature of Tuscan cooking, you will find excellent (perhaps even better) local food at the rather cheaper *ristorante* and *osteria* listed in this book. A *ristorante* corresponds very closely to the UK or US idea of a restaurant, while an *osteria* (literally an inn) is slightly more relaxed and, perhaps, rather rustic in feel.

The perfect cappuccino

In the evening, Florentines usually eat at around 8.30pm, and the best restaurants close relatively early – a contrast to the late hours typical in countries such as Spain or Portugal.

WINE

Perhaps the most famous of Italy's wines, Chianti is grown in seven regions surrounding Florence and Siena. Chianti is not just one wine, but many. In its seven zones, the variety of climates, producers and vineyards is staggering, ensuring a huge breadth of quality and complexity. The main grape here is the Sangiovese.

The heartland of Chianti lies between Florence and Siena. This is the home of Chianti Classico, where the Chianti League was formed in the 13th century, a region that produces more consistently good wine than any other zone, except for the Rufina district. The latter, the most important wine-producing region near Florence, lies in the hills above the River Sieve. It produces some of the giants of Italian wine: Selvapiana, Castello di Nipozzano, Fatoria di Vetrie and the new heavyweight, Montesodi. The region surrounding Florence itself, the Chianti Coli Fiorentina, tends to produce wines that are heavy and coarse.

Key names
Four families dominate wine production around Florence: Antinori, Frescobaldi, Guicciardini-Srozzi and Ricasoli. It is they who are responsible for the single-vineyard 'super-Tuscans', which now have such a high reputation. From Antinori look out for Sassicaia or Tignanello, or from Ricasoli try a Brolio.

Top labels to look for include Vino Nobile di Montepulciano, Brunello di Montalcino and Brolio – all red wines. Although the region's reds are by far the best-known and, for the most part, superior, wines in Chianti, light and simple whites are also out there. Most are based on Trebbiano and Malvasia grapes. The best white is generally considered to be the dry, elegant, but quite full-bodied Vernaccia di San Gimignano, from the town that lies west of Siena.

Vin Santo
The traditional way to end a classic Tuscan meal of Chianti and *bistecca alla fiorentina* is with *biscotti di Prato*, hard almond biscuits, dipped in a glass of dark gold Vin Santo (Holy Wine). This dessert wine is made from white Trebbiano and Malvasia grapes picked late, at 'the time of the saints' (around All Saints' Day, 1 November).

Food and drink prices

Throughout this book, price guide for a two-course meal for one with a glass of house wine:

€€€€ = over 60 euros
€€€ = 40–60 euros
€€ = 25–40 euros
€ = below 25 euros

Classic designs at Dolce & Gabbana

SHOPPING

High-quality goods dominate shopping in Florence, especially clothing and leather wares. Some of the best Italian designers started out in the city, and their flagship stores still line Via de' Tornabuoni.

FASHION

Alongside Milan and Rome, Florence is one of the fashion capitals of Italy. It may have an even greater claim to importance, as it was here that many of the great names of Italian fashion first opened shop. It is perhaps not surprising that many of these fashion houses first started off as makers of shoes and handbags – drawing on a long history of superb leatherwork – although almost all have now diversified to include clothing and accessories.

Designer names

One of the most famous designers, Salvatore Ferragamo, settled in Florence in 1927 and went on to fashion shoes for the most beautiful women of the century. Still one of the most prestigious and well-known luxury brands, the historic Florence flagship store is in the Palazzo Spini Feroni (Via de' Tornabuoni 4r–14r; tel: 055-292 123; www.ferragamo.com). Fans should not miss the engaging shoe museum upstairs (daily 10am–7.30pm).

The now rather flash house of Gucci (Via de' Tornabuoni 73-81r; tel: 055-264 011; www.gucci.com) was started in 1921 by the furrier Guccio Gucci. Until the 1950s it was a respectable, if somewhat staid, purveyor of handbags to the Florentine bourgeoisie. Once it had branched out onto the glamorous international market, it was picked up by style icons including Jackie Kennedy, and has not looked back since.

Dressing the well-heeled feet of Florentines for decades, home-grown Tod's classic loafers and bags come in all shapes, sizes and colours. The store is located at Via de' Tornabuoni 60r (tel: 055-219 423; www.tods.com).

Florence also has a strong history of fine textiles, and the Florentine house of Emilio Pucci capitalises on this with bold, brightly coloured prints that evoke the 1960s. They can be found at Via de' Tornabuoni 20-22r (tel: 055-265 8082; www.emiliopucci.com).

LEATHER AND TEXTILES

Leather goods are not, of course, only available from the big-name international brands. Very high-quality bags and shoes by local artisans can be found all over the city. Other good places at the top end are Bottega Fiorentina (Borgo

Marbled paper at Il Torchio   *Mary-Janes, Florence style*

dei Greci 5r; tel: 055-295 411; www. bottegafiorentina.it) and Il Bisonte (Via del Parione 31-33r; tel: 055-215 722; www.ilbisonte.com). Otherwise, head for the myriad stalls of San Lorenzo market, where you can pick up cheaper, but still well-made, leather items.

Much of the wealth of the city was based on trade, especially that of textiles. It is still possible to buy exquisite fabrics in the city, and one of the best places, especially for silks, is Antico Setificio Fiorentino (Via L. Bartolini 4; tel: 055-213 861; www. anticosetificiofiorentino.com), established in 1786. Also take a look at Casa dei Tessuti (Via de' Pecori 20-24r; tel: 055-215 961; www.casadeitessuti.com).

PAPER

Florence has been a major centre of hand-printing and bookbinding for cen-turies. Shops sell specialised stationery as well as frames and albums covered in handmade marbled paper.

Il Torchio (Via de' Bardi 17; tel: 055-234 2862; www.legatoriailtor chio.com) makes marbled paper to a secret recipe in its workshop, and also sells finely made leather and paper desk accessories.

OPENING TIMES

Traditionally shop opening times are Mon–Sat 8.30/9am–1/1.30pm and 3.30/4–7.30/8pm. Some places are closed on Monday morning or open only in the morning on Saturday. Department stores and other city-centre shops stay open all day, and there is limited opening on Sunday. All shops usually stay open later in summer.

Florence is known for its quality leather goods

Florence by night

ENTERTAINMENT

With a healthy season of opera, concerts, chamber recitals and ballet,
Florence puts up a good showing of the performing arts. If you just fancy
a drink, however, there are also some great places for a cocktail or aperitivo.

For such a small city, Florence has an exceptional programme of internationally renowned classical musicians coming to perform, principally at the city's major festival of Maggio Musicale or as part of the Teatro della Pergola's season of chamber music. In terms of nightlife, however, the scene is fairly low-key, mostly centred around a number of chic bars in the centre of town.

MUSIC, OPERA AND DANCE

The Maggio Musicale

The Maggio Musicale festival, held from May to the end of June, is the big musical event in Florence, with top names in opera, music and ballet performing in various theatres throughout the city. The main venue is the Opera di Firenze (see page 120), which these days styles itself as the Teatro del Maggio Musicale Fiorentino.

Opera and dance

The main opera and ballet season at the Opera di Firenze/Maggio Musicale Fiorentino opens around the middle of September and runs through

to Christmas. International performers and scenographers appear regularly, particularly in operatic productions. The Florence Dance Festival (www.florencedancefestival.org) held around July (dates vary), features well-known international and Italian names, along with up-and-coming dancers and choreographers.

Chamber music

The principal venue for quality chamber-music concerts in Florence is the Teatro della Pergola (see page 120), inaugurated in 1656 and a superb example of a 17th-century theatre. These concerts, which are run by the Amici della Musica and feature world-famous chamber groups and singers, are generally held at weekends. They are usually well publicised.

THEATRE

Florence is a great place for varied theatre, ranging from the classical season at Teatro della Pergola to contemporary and fringe productions at tiny venues. Most productions are in Italian but the Teatro Puccini (see

Cocktails at Colle Bereto Caffè

page 120) is worth a visit for its Fascist-era architecture.

CINEMA

Most foreign films shown in Florence are dubbed into Italian, but there are a few cinemas that show original versions, including the Odeon (see page 121) and the occasional film festival that will use subtitles rather than dubbing. There are some open-air screenings in summer.

NIGHTLIFE

Italians enjoy going out and Florence has numerous bars, including atmospheric *enoteche* (wine bars) where you can sample regional wines by the glass. The preprandial *aperitivo* has become a way of life. The price of a cocktail may seem steep but often a whole buffet is included in the price, providing a cheap alternative to dining in a restaurant.

Nightclubs are not as popular and tend to be located out of town, although in summer more open up to cater for tourists and foreign students. There are a number of English, Irish and Scottish pubs in the city, often showing Sky Sports.

The pedestrian heart of the city, with its floodlit buildings, is ideal for *la passeggiata*, the Italian custom of taking a stroll in the evening. Piazza della Repubblica, with its historic cafés and street musicians, is a hive of activity; other lively spots are Piazza Santa Croce and, on the other side of the river, Piazza Santo Spirito. Ponte Vecchio, with its river views, is a romantic spot to end the day.

A night out in town

Siege of Florence (1530), by Giorgio Vasari

HISTORY: KEY DATES

Florence has seen more than its fair share of history, from the Etruscans to the Renaissance and conflicts between the Pope and the Holy Roman Emperor, to the Risorgimento that brought modern Italy into being.

BEGINNINGS

4th C BC   Fiesole is well-established as a powerful Etruscan city.

351BC   Etruria is conquered by the Romans.

59BC   Foundation of the Roman colony of Florentia.

AD 250   The martyrdom of St Minias, to whom a shrine is dedicated on what is now the site of San Miniato church. This is the first evidence of Christianity in Florence.

4th C   Building of Santa Reparata, the city's first cathedral.

1125   Florence conquers and destroys neighbouring Fiesole.

13th C   Embroiled in factional conflicts, Florence sides with the Guelf (pro-pope) party against Ghibelline (pro-emperor) cities, such as Pisa and Siena.

1260   Siena defeats Florence at the battle of Montaperti.

1302   Dante is expelled from Florence and begins to write *The Divine Comedy*.

1322   Completion of the Palazzo Vecchio.

1348   The Black Death kills three-fifths of the Florentine population over the next 50 years. This inspires Boccaccio to write his *Decameron*.

1384   The Florentines capture Arezzo.

THE RENAISSANCE

1400–1   A competition is held to design new doors for the Baptistry; this is regarded as the start of the *rinascita* (rebirth) or Renaissance.

1406   Florence conquers Pisa and gains a sea port.

1434   Cosimo de' Medici turns the city into an artistic and intellectual centre.

1469   Cosimo's grandson Lorenzo de' Medici assumes power.

1494   Savonarola declares Florence a republic ruled only by God.

1498   Execution of Savonarola.

1512   Florence is defeated by an invading Spanish army, which facilitates the return of the Medici.

1527   Florence expels the Medici again, and reverts to a republic.

1530   Pope Clement VII and Emperor Charles V besiege Florence.

The aftermath of the 1966 flood

1531   Florence falls.
1570   Cosimo I is appointed Grand Duke of Tuscany.

1610   Cosimo II appoints Galileo as court mathematician.
1631   Galileo is excommunicated.

FOREIGN RULE AND INDEPENDENCE

1737   The last Medici grand duke dies without an heir and the title passes to the Austrian House of Lorraine.
1808   France annexes Tuscany.
1848   Tuscany is a vanguard in the first Italian War of Independence.
1865   Florence becomes the temporary capital of the emerging united Italy.
1919   Benito Mussolini founds the Italian Fascist Party.
1939–45   During World War II, the Nazis destroy parts of central Florence. The Ponte Vecchio is the only old bridge to survive the war.
1946   Italy becomes a republic.
1966   Florence is flooded by the River Arno and many works of art are lost.
1988   Florentines vote to exclude traffic and to control air pollution.
1993   A Mafia bomb kills five people and damages the Uffizi gallery.

THE 21ST CENTURY

2002   The euro replaces the lira as the unit of currency in Italy.
2002–3   Michelangelo's *David* is restored.
2010   Opening of Line 1 of the long-awaited Tramvia (tram line).
2012   After a 32-year restoration Ghiberti's 'Gate of Paradise' are unveiled. Work begins on Norman Foster's TAV railway station.
2014   Former Mayor of Florence and Democratic Party leader Matteo Renzi becomes Italy's prime minister. Dario Nardella succeeds him as the city's new mayor.
2015   Florence hosts a number of events connected to Milan-held EXPO 2015.

2016   Florence's oldest theatre, the Teatro Niccolini, reopens, fully restored, after a 20-year closure.
2018   The Uffizi Gallery sees a record number of visitors with numbers reaching over four million.

Crowds at the Uffizi

BEST ROUTES

The Duomo and Campanile

PIAZZA DEL DUOMO

At the heart of this impressive square is one of the largest cathedrals in the world. Notable for both art and architecture, the Duomo and the museum associated with it give a fine introduction to the city.

DISTANCE: 1km (0.5mile)
TIME: A half day
START: Piazza del Duomo
END: Museo dell'Opera del Duomo
POINTS TO NOTE: It may be best to avoid doing this route on a Sunday, when the opening hours for the Duomo are restricted. In peak season expect lengthy queues; purchasing a Firenze Card (€85) enables you to skip the queues at the Duomo, dome and bell tower. It is valid for 72 hours, gives priority admission to as many as 76 museums and is available at 11 authorised points of sale throughout the city and online (www.firenzecard.it).

The grandest monument in Florence is undoubtedly the great dome of Brunelleschi's cathedral. Along with the bell tower designed by Giotto, it dominates the city skyline and, like Michelangelo's sculpture of David, is considered to be a symbol of the city. The square in which it sits is also home to the cathedral's Baptistry, whose doors are some of the greatest achievements of early Renaissance sculpture. The spectacle of the Duomo, Campanile and Baptistry, particularly now with the pedestrianisation of the piazza, never fails to impress.

PIAZZA DEL DUOMO

The walk starts at the western end of **Piazza del Duomo**, where it adjoins Piazza di San Giovanni. The best place for kick-starting your day with a strong black espresso and perhaps a small cake or savoury snack is at one of the cafés located on the two squares. Most have seats outside that offer good views of the majestic cathedral dome and the adjoining bell tower. A good option is **Scudieri**, see ①. From here you can get a sense of the huge scale of the cathedral, once the largest church in Christendom, and still the fourth biggest in the world (after St Peter's in Rome, St Paul's in London and the cathedral in Milan, also called the Duomo).

Angelic detail in the Baptistry

The whole experience of sitting down having a coffee in Piazza del Duomo has become a much more relaxed and tranquil affair since Florence's former mayor, Matteo Renzi (and later Italy's prime minister), banned vehicles of any description in the square, horses and carriages included.

From the café, walk round to the front of the cathedral and join the queue outside the left-hand door to get in.

THE DUOMO

The Cattedrale di Santa Maria del Fiore is most commonly known as **Il Duomo** ❶ (www.museumflorence.com; Mon–Sat 10am–4.30pm, Sun 1.30–4.45pm), which comes from the Latin *Domus Dei*, meaning House of God. It was built as a place of worship but, just as importantly, it symbolised the ambition and pride of the city at a time when it led the world in art, science and philosophy. The cathedral took almost 150 years to build (from 1294 to 1436), but the neo-Gothic façade, the exuberance of which contrasts with the sober restraint of the buildings surrounding the square, was not added until the 19th century.

The façade

The original façade for the Duomo was designed by Arnolfo di Cambio (d.1302), who had worked with Niccolò Pisano on the pulpit for Siena Cathedral. It took the historicising trend of the late 19th century to actually complete the job with a neo-Romanesque design by Emilio de Fabris.

The top of the Duomo

The crypt of Santa Reparata

Inside, the steps to the right lead down to the crypt (www.museumflorence. com; Mon−Wed, Fri 10am−5pm, Thu−Sat until 4.30pm, closed Sun; combined ticket). Here, you will find Brunelleschi's simple grave: the inscription on the tomb slab compares him to Icarus, the mythical hero who learned to fly but then plunged to his death when he flew too close to the sun and it melted his wings. Brunelleschi's is the only tomb in the cathedral (although there are various memorials); his burial within its walls was a singular honour granted in recognition of his genius in building the dome. The rest of the crypt contains the ancient ruins of Santa Reparata, the church which was demolished to make way for the Duomo.

Notable artworks

Turn left out of the crypt and right along the cathedral's north wall. You will pass a fresco of Sir John Hawkwood on horseback, painted by Paolo Uccello in 1436. Hawkwood was an English *condottiere* (mercenary), whose hired soldiers often fought for Florence. Other cities honoured military heroes with equestrian statues in stone or bronze; the fact that Hawkwood was commemorated only in a fresco is often cited as an example of Florentine miserliness.

Nearby, you will also see a painting of Dante outside the walls of Florence,

symbolising his exile. The picture was commissioned in 1465 to commemorate the bicentenary of the poet's birth. Probably Florence's greatest writer, Dante Aligheri (c.1265−1321) was a supporter of the Guelfi Bianci (White Guelfs), who demanded more freedom from Rome. They were defeated by the Guelfi Neri (Black Guelfs) in 1301, and Dante, who was in Rome at the time, found himself in exile. In 1302, after refusing to pay a fine, he was sentenced to death by burning if he returned to Florence. This order was finally lifted in 2008, when the city's Commune (government) passed a motion to revoke the sentence.

Ahead lies the sanctuary, with its lovely (mainly 15th-century) stained-glass windows. Soaring high above is the restored fresco of the *Last Judgement* painted by Vasari in 1572−9 on the underside of the dome. Vasari intended these scenes to rival the work of Michelangelo in the Sistine Chapel in Rome, but the cartoon-like scenes of devils dragging their victims to hell by the testicles do not quite match Michelangelo's more profound vision of eternal damnation.

The dome

The cathedral's soaring central dome was built by Filippo Brunelleschi (1377−1446), the greatest architect and engineer of his day. As a tribute to Brunelleschi, no other edifice in

Duomo detail

The octagonal Baptistry

Florence has been built as high as the dome since its completion in 1436, when the cathedral was consecrated by Pope Eugenius IV.

The external gallery that partially runs around the bottom of one section of the dome was designed by Baccio d'Agnolo in around 1506. It was originally intended to pass all the way around but work on the gallery ceased in 1515, when Michelangelo referred to it disparagingly as a 'cricket's cage'.

Climbing the dome

For a closer look at these vast and impressive figures, you can climb up to the dome (www.museumflorence.com; Mon–Fri 8.30am–7pm, Sat 8.30am–5pm, Sun 1–4pm; combined ticket). To do so, exit the cathedral and circle round to the right to the Porta della Mandoria on the north side, from where you can then make the ascent.

You need stamina to tackle the 463 spiralling steps to the top of the dome, but you will be rewarded by intimate glimpses of its construction on the way up, and a fabulous view of the city once you reach the top. Climbers descending the stairs frequently pass encouraging remarks to those still arduously toiling upwards.

Before Brunelleschi, nobody had built such a huge dome since Roman times; he visited Rome to study the 2nd-century AD Pantheon in order to reinvent the ancient technique of building upwards in decreasing circles of interlocking brick. On the way up you pass between the dome's two shells. The inner one of brick, laid in a herringbone fashion, is virtually self-supporting and provided a platform for the scaffolding on which the outer shell was constructed.

The Campanile

If you have walked to the top of the dome, you may not have the inclination to also climb the 414 steps of the **Campanile di Giotto** ❷ (www.museumflorence.com; daily 8.15am–6.50pm; combined ticket), on the left as you leave the cathedral. The bell tower, was designed by Giotto in 1331, six years before his death, but only completed in 1359. The view from the top, however, is just as spectacular as that from the dome.

LOGGIA DEL BIGALLO

On the southern side of the piazza, opposite the Baptistry, is the Loggia del Bigallo. This was built between 1352 and 1358, and features some fine International Gothic decoration. It now contains a small museum (Mon–Sat tours: 10am, noon, 3pm; Sun tours: 10am, noon; reservations necessary; tel: 055-288 496), showcasing a number of artworks. Most famous of these is Bernardo's Daddi's fresco of the Madonna della Mis-

'Gate of Paradise' detail

ericordia, in which the earliest-known view of Florence is found (1342).

In the 14th century, unwanted babies used to be left on the porch of the Loggia del Bigallo; if they were not claimed within three days, they would be sent to foster homes.

THE BAPTISTRY

Walk over to the little octagonal **Battistero** ③ (www.museumflorence. com; Mon–Fri 8.15–10.15am and

The Baptistry's magnificent bronze doors

11.15am–7.30pm, Sat 8.15–6.30pm, Sun 8.15–1.30pm; combined ticket) to the west of the cathedral. Florentines have always exaggerated the antiquity of the Baptistry. Evidence suggests that it was built in the 6th or 7th century using Roman masonry. In the 12th century it was taken under the wing of the Calimala, the guild of wool importers, who paid for its marble cladding of green geometric designs on a white background, an innovative design admired and imitated elsewhere in Tuscany (the Duomo also follows its example).

Baptistry doors
Set into this 10th-century building, one of the city's oldest, are three sets of bronze doors (all casts of the originals). Those to the south were made in the 1330s by the Pisan artist Andrea Pisano and illustrate the Life of St John the Baptist, the patron saint of Florence. Although they are early works, the dynamism in the dramatic grouping of figures, and the fluency and immediacy of his style contrast with the static spirituality of 13th- and 14th-century Gothic art. Pisano was several decades ahead of his time.

Perhaps even more important are the later sets of doors by Lorenzo Ghiberti (see box) that illustrate Old Testament scenes (the originals, completed in 1452, are displayed in the Museo dell'Opera del Duomo, see page 33). The door frames, which

Mosaics in the dome at the Baptistry

are original, contain portrait busts of 24 leading Renaissance artists; Ghiberti himself is the bald-headed figure, third up from the bottom in the centre of the doors.

The interior
Inside the Baptistry, the ceiling is covered in striking mosaics that depict the main events of the Old and New Testaments. Executed in sparkling gold, ruby and turquoise glass cubes, they are the work of various 13th-century artists. Beneath the dome are the remains of the pavement of 1209, inlaid with the signs of the Zodiac. Two Roman columns have been incorporated into the graceful marble cladding of the walls to the right of the altar, where they flank the beautiful marble tomb of Pope John XXIII, with its bronze effigy of the sleeping pope by Donatello (1425). The Pope died on a visit to Florence in 1419.

By this time you may feel in need of a little refreshment before carrying on. One option is to try the fabulous ice-creams at **Grom**, see ②, or, for something more substantial, visit the nearby **Fiaschetteria Nuvoli**, see ③.

MUSEO DELL'OPERA DEL DUOMO

Now walk back to the Duomo and carry on around its northern side, towards the eastern end of the Piazza del Duomo. At the far end of the square is the **Museo dell'Opera del Duomo** ❹

(Museum of the Cathedral's Artefacts; www.museumflorence.com; daily 9am–7.30pm; combined ticket). The museum is located within a building erected by Brunelleschi in 1432 as the base from which he supervised

Ghiberti's doors
The Renaissance proper is conventionally dated to 1401, when a competition was held to select an artist for the remaining two sets of doors for the Baptistry. Of the seven artists who applied, the winner, Lorenzo Ghiberti (1378–1455), first made the doors for the north entrance that illustrate New Testament scenes (1424). He then made the superb 'Gate of Paradise' (Porta del Paradiso) for the east entrance, so called because Michelangelo declared they were fitting enough for the entrance to heaven. If anything, however, it was Brunelleschi's losing submission that truly indicated that the Renaissance had arrived: his trial piece was more logical in layout and, in its depiction of the actors in the drama, less idealised and more concerned with the human drama of the story than those of Ghiberti. It depicts Abraham raising the knife to Isaac's head and, just in time, the angel grasps Abraham's wrist and points to the sheep now in his view. The original bronze panel can now be seen in the Bargello (see page 48).

Entrance to the Museo dell'Opera del Duomo

the construction of the great cathedral dome. The museum encompasses 25 rooms over three floors and displays over 750 works of art, including a number of outstanding works of sculpture from the cathedral and the campanile, many of which have been brought indoors to protect them from atmospheric pollution and weathering.

The ground floor

On the ground floor the grandest addition to the museum is the Salone del Paradiso. One of its walls is entirely covered by the monumental reconstruction of the earliest façade of Santa Maria del Fiore, never completed and finally dismantled in 1587, while the opposite wall showcases the original 10 panels from the Baptistry 'Gate of Paradise' by Lorenzo Ghiberti (see page 33).

The next room of note is the Salla della Maddalena, which centres around Donatello's *Mary Magdalene*, a figure of penitence carved in wood, and other sculptures and paintings representing saints.

The adjacent Tribuna di Michelangelo is devoted to Michelangelo's *Pietà*, begun in around 1550 and originally intended to adorn his own tomb. The hooded figure at the centre of the group is a self-portrait; Michelangelo cast himself as Nicodemus, the rich man who donated his tomb for the burial of Christ. The rather stiff

figure of Mary Magdalene, to the left, was carved by one of Michelangelo's pupils. Dissatisfied with his work, the great master broke up the *Pietà*; it survived only because a servant kept the pieces.

The first floor

One of the most interesting rooms on the first floor is the Galleria della Cupola, which evokes the various stages of construction of the dome by Filippo Brunelleschi's team with 15th-century wood models and a selection of period tools.

Beyond is the Sala delle Cantorie, showcasing two fine *cantorie* (choir galleries) carved in marble that were removed from the cathedral during the 17th century. Both depict young musicians in a frenzy of dancing and music-making. They were made by two of the leading artists of the day, Donatello and Luca della Robbia, between 1431 and 1438.

Next room of note is the Sala del Tesoro, which displays the Cathedral's treasures including a 14th-century altar front and a monumental cross of pure silver from the Baptistry.

The second floor

On the second floor, the Galleria dei Modeli presents seven wood models illustrating proposals for a Renaissance façade to replace the medieval one demolished in 1587 (and reconstructed on the ground floor in the

Inside the Museo

Salone del Paradiso).

Don't miss the Belvedere della Cupola – its skylight offers an unusual view of the dome.

If you began your tour around lunchtime, it may well be time for an *aperitivo*. A short walk to the south of the museum on Borgo degli Albizi is a great bar, **I Visacci**, see ④.

DONATELLO'S WORKSHOP

Around the corner from where Michelangelo carved his *David*, was where another great Renaissance sculptor, Donatello (1386–1466), had his workshop. Almost next door to the museum, look for the building, which is now occupied by a restaurant named after the artist.

Food and drink

① SCUDIERI
Piazza di San Giovanni 19r; tel: 055-210 733; daily 7am–11pm;
€€
A long-standing and rather grand café situated close to the Baptistry and perfect for a – rather expensive – breakfast or snack. The chocolate-based patisserie is excellent, and the prices are worth it for the location and surroundings.

② GROM
Via del Campanile; tel: 055-216 158; www. grom.it; daily 10.30am–10.30pm;
€
This chain of artisan *gelaterie* started in Turin and has quickly become a favourite in Florence. Located to the south of the bell tower, on the corner of Via delle Oche, Grom's ice cream contains only fresh and in-season organic fruit, with no colourings. Mineral water is used as a base for sorbets, and high-quality whole milk and organic eggs for the creams. Check out the monthly flavours and suggested pairings. Also worth trying is the almond granita.

③ FIASCHETTERIA NUVOLI
Piazza dell'Olio 15r; tel: 055-239 6616; Mon–Sat 8am–9pm, Sun 9.30am–5.30pm; €
Situated just behind the Baptistry, this tiny eatery serves up Florentine specialities daily. Enjoy a sandwich and sip a glass of wine on the stools out front, or head downstairs, where you will find rustic seating and friendly Tuscan waiters. A much-needed inexpensive option in an otherwise overpriced area, it is very popular, and you might consider reserving ahead.

④ I VISACCI
Borgo degli Albizi 80r; tel: 055-263 9443; daily 4pm–3am; €
A colourful café that serves drinks and light lunches and offers more than pasta, pizza or panini: choose from the *crostini*, salads or fish- or meat-based plates. Very relaxed ambience and friendly staff. Particularly good for a pre-prandial cocktail, and, later on, a DJ livens the bar up.

Palazzo Vecchio

ORSANMICHELE TO THE PONTE VECCHIO

The impressive space of Piazza della Signoria is arguably the heart of the city. Witness to many upheavals throughout history, it is overlooked by the towering Palazzo Vecchio, formerly the ancestral home of the Medici.

DISTANCE: 1km (0.5 mile)
TIME: A half day
START: Orsanmichele
END: Ponte Vecchio
POINTS TO NOTE: If you are in a hurry to pack in the sights, it is possible to link this route with route no. 3 of the Uffizi Gallery. However, this would make for a very long day of sightseeing and possible art fatigue. On its own, this walk works well as an afternoon tour.

This route explores the area around the political centre of medieval Florence, the expansive Piazza della Signoria. This is the location of Michelangelo's iconic *David*, as well as the Palazzo Vecchio, once the home of the Medici rulers and now the city's town hall.

If you want to grab some lunch first, head for **Ristorante Paoli**, see ❶, on Via dei Tavolini, just opposite where the route begins outside Orsanmichele.

ORSANMICHELE

Start your walk in Via de'Calzaiuoli outside the church of **Orsanmichele** ❶ (Tue–Sun 10am–5pm).

Orsanmichele was built in 1337 on the site of the garden *(hortus)* of the monastery church of San Michele, and the combination of the two words gives its present name. Originally it served as an open-arcaded grain market but in 1380 the arcades were filled in and the ground floor converted to a church, while the upper storey became an emergency grain store to be used in times of siege or famine. This is a small museum (open Monday only 10am–5pm) housing original statuary from the church.

Walk round the church, to the right, and down Via Orsanmichele, where you can study the statues in the wall niches. Each of these niches belonged to one of the city's powerful guilds, who commissioned artists to portray their patron saints. The most famous statue, Donatello's *St George*, is now replaced by a copy; the original

Outside Orsanmichele   *Imposing Orsanmichele tower*

can be seen in the Bargello (see page 48).

The interior

At the back of the church, an aerial corridor links Orsanmichele to the 13th-century **Palazzo del'Arte della Lana** (Wool Guild Palace). The entrance to the church is located just beneath the corridor.

The centrepiece of this astonishingly rich Gothic church is Andrea Orcagna's elaborate tabernacle (1459), which is decorated with scenes from the *Life of the Virgin*, and encloses Bernardo Daddi's painting of the *Madonna* (1347).

Turn left out of the church, left again in Via de' Lamberti, passing Donatello's statue of *St Mark* in the first niche, then right in Via de' Calzaiuoli, to **Piazza della Signoria ➋**.

PIAZZA DELLA SIGNORIA

This handsome square was long a place of political strife. The land and buildings were owned by the Uberti, supporters of the Ghibelline (imperial) faction, losers to the Guelf (papal) party in the struggles that tore Florence apart in the 13th century. The property of the exiled Uberti was first left to crumble as a sign of the family's defeat, but then chosen as the site of a new palace to house the city government.

Towering over everything is the battlemented façade and campanile of the Palazzo Vecchio, which was built to house the government between 1299 and 1322. It dwarfs even the huge heroic figure of **David ➌** (a copy – Michelangelo's original is in the Accademia, see page 60), Bandinelli's rather lumpy figure of *Hercules* (1534) and the licentious nymphs of Ammanati's **Fontana**

Palazzo Vecchio coat of arms

di Nettuno 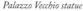 ❹ (Neptune Fountain; 1575). These works of art, all fronting the palace, symbolise Florence in various ways: for example, David representing a figure of defiance against tyranny; Hercules, the mythical founder of the city; and Neptune being a metaphor for the city's naval fleet, created by Cosimo I.

Also in front of the palazzo is a *marzocco* – a heraldic lion bearing the city's arms (the symbol of Florence) – has graced the piazza for almost as long as the palazzo itself. What you see today is a copy; the original is in the Bargello.

Palazzo Vecchio statue

The Loggia of the Lancers
To the right of the Palazzo Vecchio is the **Loggia dei Lanzi** ❺. Originally a covered vantage point for city officials at public ceremonies, it took its later name from Cosimo I's Swiss-German mercenary bodyguards, known as *Landsknechts* (Italianised to *Lanzichenecchi*), who used it as a guardroom during his nine-year residence in the Palazzo Vecchio.

Since the late 18th century the loggia has officially been an open-air sculpture museum, but celebrated works of art have been displayed here since long before then. Cellini's fine bronze *Perseus* was originally placed here, on Cosimo's order in 1554. Giambologna's famous *Rape of the Sabine Women* was added in 1583, while his *Hercules and the Centaur* and the Roman statues at the back, donated by the Medici, were added towards the end of the 18th century.

Before entering the Palazzo Vecchio you might like to take some refreshment. One option, on the square itself, is the classy **Rivoire**, see ❷, with its ice cream, pastries and views of the historic buildings.

PALAZZO VECCHIO

Climb the steps of the **Palazzo Vecchio** ❻ (www.museicivicifiorentini.comune.fi.it; Fri–Wed 9am–7pm, until 11pm Apr–Sept; Thu 9am–2pm).

The palace was completely remodelled when Cosimo moved into it in 1540, having quashed republicanism

'Rape of the Sabine Women'   *Inside the former home of the Medici*

in Florence and established himself as an hereditary duke. Politicians have addressed the public from the front of the Palazzo Vecchio since the 14th century. Originally, this was done from the raised platform, the *ringheria* (which gave rise to the term 'to harangue'), until it was demolished in 1812.

The name of the building has changed almost as often as power in the city has changed hands. From the Palazzo del Popolo – the People's Palace – it became the Palazzo della Signoria when the *signori*, the heads of the leading families, took over the reins of government. It then became the Palazzo Ducale when Cosimo moved in. In 1550, the Pitti Palace became the duke's new official residence and from that time the building has been known as the Palazzo Vecchio, the Old Palace.

The palace is now partly a museum, partly the town hall, where the citizens of Florence come to arrange birth and death certificates, pay their fines and get married. It is not unusual to get caught-up in a rice-throwing wedding party while viewing the inner courtyards.

To the right of the Palazzo Vecchio's main entrance, just behind the statue of Hercules, is the profile of a man scratched into the stone. It is attributed to Michelangelo.

The courtyard
You enter via a *cortile* (courtyard), designed in 1453 by Michelozzo Michelozzi. The little fountain in the

centre was designed by Giorgio Vasari, court architect from 1555–74, who also produced the frescoes and stucco in the surrounding arcade.

On the walls are views of Austrian cities, painted to make Joanna of Austria

Savonarola

Girolamo Savonarola (1452–98) was appointed as the hard-line Prior of San Marco in 1491. Under Charles VIII of France he became the leader of Florence in 1494 and ruled over the city for four years, convinced that he was an agent of God, sent to punish Florentines for their obsession with pagan philosophies, secular books and profane art. Among the draconian laws he imposed was the punishment of death for wearing 'lewd' clothes. As part of his fanatical obsession with creating a city prepared for the Apocalypse he instigated a 'bonfire of the vanities'. For this, he and his supporters collected anything they considered immoral or pagan, including a large number of works of art – among them paintings by Botticelli – and burnt them on a large pyre in Piazza della Signoria. After this, public opinion turned against him, especially when he was excommunicated and the threat of papal rule fell over the city. He was executed in 1498, and a plaque on the pavement near the Neptune Fountain marks the spot in Piazza della Signoria where he was burnt to death.

feel at home when she married Francesco de' Medici (Cosimo's son) in 1565. The ceiling is covered in grotesque figures in imitation of the ancient Roman paintings in the grotto of Nero's garden in Rome. Next to the ticket office, the new Tracce di Firenze (Traces of Florence) exhibition presents a pictorial history of the city, from the Middle Ages to the 20th century.

Room of the Five Hundred

The state chambers start on the first floor with the Salone dei Cinquecento (Room of the Five Hundred). This was designed in 1495 for the 500-strong ruling assembly – the Consiglio Maggiore – of the penultimate republic. It was the largest room of its time. Despite its appalling acoustics, the vast space is now used occasionally as a concert hall.

Leonardo da Vinci and Michelangelo were both commissioned to paint the walls and ceilings of the Salone dei Cinquecento, but neither got much further than experimental sketches. It was left to Vasari to undertake the work, which was executed with great speed between 1563 and 1565. Nominally, the paintings celebrate the foundation of Florence and the recent victories over its rivals, Pisa and Siena. The ubiquitous presence of Cosimo I in all the scenes, however, makes it simply a vast exercise in ducal propaganda.

It is not unusual for visitors to feel uneasy and wonder why Vasari stooped to such overt flattery. Michelangelo's *The Genius of Victory* is equally disturbing. Brutally realistic, it depicts an old man who has been forced to the ground by the superior strength of a muscular youth. It was carved for the tomb of Julius II in Rome, but Michelangelo's heirs presented it to Cosimo I to commemorate the 1559 victory over Siena. The artist intended it to represent the triumph of reason over ignorance, but in this context it seems part of a gross celebration of war. Even so, artists have frequently sought to imitate Michelangelo's twisted, tortured figures, and it was one of the works most admired by the later 16th-century Mannerists.

Light relief is provided by another 16th-century work, *Hercules and Diomedes* of Vincenzo de' Rossi, a no-holds-barred tussle, in which the inverted Diomedes takes revenge by squeezing Hercules' genitals in a pain-inducing grip.

Other first-floor highlights

Off the main hall is the study (**Studiolo**) of the reclusive Francesco I (usually only accessible on a guided tour), built between 1570 and 1575. The beautiful cupboards were used to store his treasures and the equipment for his experiments in alchemy. His parents, Cosimo I and Eleonora di Toledo, are depicted in the wall frescoes by Bronzino. Other paintings depict the four elements.

Next in sequence comes the suite of rooms known as the Quartiere di Leone

X, decorated in 1556–62 by Vasari and named after Giovanni de' Medici, son of Lorenzo the Magnificent, who was created a cardinal at the age of 13 and eventually became Pope Leo X.

Quarters of the Elements

On the floor above is the **Quartiere degli Elementi** (once again by Vasari), with allegories of the elements, including a watery scene reminiscent of the work of Botticelli. The corner room, the Terrazza di Saturno, provides fine views east to Santa Croce and south to San Miniato, while in another small room is Verrocchio's original *Boy with Dolphin* (1470).

Quarters of Eleonor of Toledo

The **Quartiere di Eleonora di Toledo**, the private rooms of the beautiful wife of Cosimo I include the chapel. A masterpiece of Florentine Mannerism, it is adorned with stunning frescoes by Bronzino (1540–5), and offers a rare opportunity to study fresco work at close quarters. The sheer range and brilliance of the colour is striking, with hues that are rarely seen in modern painting.

Eleonora's bedroom is decorated with a frieze based on her initials, and has a lovely marble washbasin; another room is painted with domestic scenes – spinning, weaving and tasks that correspond to the classical idea of virtuous motherhood. The last room shows Florentine street scenes and festivities.

Hall of Justice and Room of the Lilies

A corridor containing the serene death mask of Dante leads to the two most sumptuous rooms of the palace, the **Sala d'Udienza** and the **Sala dei Gigli**. Both have gilded and coffered ceilings, decorated with every conceivable form of ornament. The 16th-century intarsia doors between the two depict the poets Dante and Petrarch.

The Sala dei Gigli is named after the so-called lilies (irises, in reality) that cover the walls. The frescoes are by Ghirlandaio and the ceiling by the Maiano brothers. Donatello's original *Judith and Holofernes* (1460) is the highlight here, with information panels that explain how the bronze was cast and restored.

Other second-floor highlights

The **Cancelleria**, a small chamber off to the side (entered through the remains of a 13th-century window), was built in 1511 as an office for Niccolò Machiavelli during his term as government secretary. A portrait by Santi di Tito depicts the youthful, smiling author of *The Prince,* looking nothing like the demonic figure he was branded when his study of politics and pragmatism was published.

Just off the Sala dei Gigli is the Sala delle Carte, formerly La Guardaroba (wardrobe), which contains a large 16th-century globe showing the extent of the then known world. The room is lined with wooden cupboards adorned with a remarkable series of maps.

Ponte Vecchio viewed from the north

Special tours and the Children's Museum

The **Museo dei Ragazzi** (Mus.e, Children's Museum, entry in the Via de' Gondi; www.musefirenze.it; Mon–Sat 9.30am–1pm, 2.30–5pm, Sun 9.30am–12.30pm) puts on a host of well-organised activities for children on a reservation-only basis (tel: 055-276 8224 or online). There's a Renaissance-themed playroom for three- to seven-year-olds, and actor-led workshops and tours for older children (in Italian) and parents (in English). Activities include the 'Secrets Passages' tours (Percorso Segreto; daily at various times), which take in secret passages and odd corners made for the rulers, such as the Treasury of Cosimo I and the staircase of the Duke of Athens.

GUCCI GARDEN

For light relief from Medici propaganda visit the **Gucci Garden** ❼ (Piazza Signoria; www.gucci.com; daily 10am–10.30pm) housed on two floors of the historic Palazzo della Mercanzia a stone's throw from the Palazzo Vecchio. Themed rooms designed by Alessandro Michele celebrate both the Gucci archives and the brand's contemporary history: from retro items and advertising campaigns to two rooms that render the animal and garden based narrative of the company in the recent years. The elegant Gucci Osteria da Massimo Bottura restaurant and Gucci store complete the scene.

PIAZZALE DEGLI UFFIZI AND THE PONTE VECCHIO

From Piazza della Signoria head south to the long narrow courtyard, **Piazzale degli Uffizi** ❽, that lies between the two wings of the Uffizi Gallery, covered in full in tour no. 3. Unless you have the energy to visit the gallery at this point, continue walking down to the Arno and turn right along Lungarno Archibusieri to the **Ponte Vecchio** ❾ (literally the Old Bridge).

The oldest bridge in Florence, the Ponte Vecchio is as much a symbol of the city as the Duomo, *David*, or Palazzo Vecchio. It dates, in its present form, from 1345, replacing an earlier wooden structure that was swept away in a flood. Notably, it was the only bridge in the city to be spared being bombed during World War II; legend has it that this was because of Hitler's fond memories of it.

The bridge's occupants

Workshops have always flanked the Ponte Vecchio's central carriageway, and in 1565 Vasari's Corridor was built high above the pavement along the eastern side to link the Palazzo Pitti and the Palazzo Vecchio. In 1593, Ferdinando I, annoyed at the noisy and noxious trades that were carried on beneath his feet as he travelled the length of the corridor, ordered the resident butchers, tanners and blacksmiths, who threw their waste straight into the river, to be evicted.

On the bridge

The workshops were rebuilt and let to goldsmiths, and this traditional use has continued ever since, though no craftsmen work in the cramped but quaint premises any more. Ferdinando took the opportunity to double the rent, and so to get value for money, the goldsmiths built the extensions overhanging the river at the back of their shops.

The Ponte Vecchio is now a popular place for street traders. If you are after a poster of Bob Marley or want a suspect copy of a Prada handbag, you are in luck, otherwise it is more of an irritation, as traders block the road and add another obstruction to the already congested street.

If, having finished the tour, you are looking for somewhere to eat, retrace your steps to Piazza della Signoria. Just off the top right-hand corner of the square is Via dei Magazzini, where you will find **Frescobaldi**, see ③, with good Tuscan food, or for something a bit more modern try **Gustavino**, see ④, on Via della Condotta.

Food and drink

① RISTORANTE PAOLI

Via dei Tavolini 12r; tel: 055-216 215; www.ristorantepaoli.com; daily noon–3pm, 6.30–10.30pm; €€

This historic restaurant, founded in 1824, is a good place to try traditional Tuscan cooking. The building dates back to the 14th century, but the attractive neo-Gothic interior is actually from the early 20th century. If you are popping in for lunch, then the salads are well worth a try.

② RIVOIRE

Piazza della Signoria 4r; tel: 055-214 412; www.rivoire.it; daily 7.30am–10pm; €€

A grand café located on the piazza, which is famed for its handmade chocolates and drinking chocolate. Treat yourself to a coffee or gelato during the day or a cocktail in the early evening. While it is more expensive than other places, the outside tables offer great views over the square.

③ FRESCOBALDI

Via dei Magazzini 2-4r; tel: 055-284 724; www.frescobaldifirenze.it; daily noon–1am, Nov–Mar closed from 3pm to 6pm; €€€

Tucked away, this lovely little place dishes up flavoursome Tuscan dishes to complement its huge range of local wines. Try the *porchetta* (roast suckling pig) with a glass of Chianti from the cantina. Outside seating is available during the summer months.

④ GUSTAVINO

Via di Servi 9/r; tel: 055-906 1372, www.gustavino.it; Mon–Fri 7–11.30pm, Sat–Sun 12.30–3.30pm and 7–11.30pm; €€€

The food at this glossy restaurant is creative without being over-fussy, and is beautifully presented. Look out for the speciality wine-and-food evenings they run.

THE UFFIZI

Quite simply, this is the world's greatest collection of Italian Renaissance art, beautifully housed in a U-shaped 16th-century building whose former use as the administrative centre for the Medici family gave it its name, 'The Offices'.

TIME: A full day
POINTS TO NOTE: To avoid huge queues book advance tickets through Firenze Musei (www.firenzemusei.it). The Firenze Card (see page 122) also enables you to skip the queues. Expect considerably higher prices when temporary exhibitions are held.

A visit to the **Galleria degli Uffizi** (www.uffizi.it; www.virtualuffizi.com; Tue–Sun 8.15am–6.50pm) is a memorable experience. Here are some of the most famous works of art ever made and the breadth of the Italian collections, including pieces by Giotto, Botticelli, Leonardo, Raphael and Michelangelo, is astounding.

The Uffizi is unique in that most of its paintings were created in Florence, by Florentine artists, for Florentine patrons. Many were commissioned, collected or inherited by the Medici, whose last surviving family member, Anna Maria Ludovica, bequeathed the

entire collection to the citizens of Florence upon her death in 1743.

THE BUILDING

The ticket office for the gallery is located in the long, narrow courtyard of Piazzale degli Uffizi. The courtyard is always thronged with people and unless you have booked tickets in advance, you will have to join the queue.

The Uffizi itself was built in 1560 by the court architect, Giorgio Vasari (1511–74) to provide offices *(uffici)* for the Medici administration. The building has always been used by the Medici to display prize works of art from their collections, including numerous Roman and Greek statues.

Layout

The main collection is on the second floor, with four further rooms located on the first floor and temporary exhibitions held on the ground floor.

The Uffizi has been undergoing a massive and painfully slow redevelopment since 1989, and the work is far

The gallery backs onto the Arno

from complete. The Nuovi Uffizi project will double the number of paintings on show and allow twice as many visitors to the gallery. Some ideas, however, have not been without controversy, especially the avant-garde design for a new exit by the Japanese architect Arata Isozaki, which has been at a standstill since 2003. During renovations many works of art have been rearranged or moved to different galleries.

THE SECOND FLOOR

Begin on the second floor, where rooms 2 to 4 are dedicated to works from Siena and Florence during the pre-Renaissance Duecento and Trecento (13th and 14th centuries). Notable pieces

here include Cimabue's late 12th-century *Maestà* (or Virgin Enthroned) and his pupil Giotto's *Ognissanti Madonna* (1310). These contrast with the more conservative works of the later International Gothic (rooms 5 and 6) although some of these are still exquisite, particularly Lorenzo Monaco's *Coronation of the Virgin Mary* (1414).

The early Renaissance

Room 7 is dedicated to the founders and leading figures of the early Renaissance, who explored purely secular subjects for the first time in Western art since antiquity. Uccello's *Battle of San Remo* (1456) celebrates the Florentine victory over long-time rivals, the Sienese. Other artists here include Masaccio – see especially his *Madonna and Child with St Anne* (1424) – and Fra Angelico.

The Filippo Lippi Room (8) holds the Franciscan monk's lovely mid-15th-century *Madonna and Child with Two Angels*, which is notable for its realistic treatment of landscape. Also here are Piero della Francesca's honest portraits of the *Duke and Duchess of Urbino I* (*c*.1465) in all their ugly glory.

The Botticelli Rooms (10 to 14) are the most popular, containing the world's best collection of work by the artist. Highlights include the mythological paintings – the *Birth of Venus* (*c*.1485) and *Primavera* (*c*.1480) – which fused ideas of the spiritual and the secular. The meaning of the latter remains a subject of ardent discussion, while the figure of Venus has overtones of the Virgin Mary.

The High Renaissance

The High Renaissance arrives with room 15. On show are early paintings by Leonardo da Vinci, including the *Annunciation* (1475) and the unfinished *Adoration of the Magi* (1482), as well as works by Perugino and Signorelli.

The Tribuna (room 18) is an octagonal room lit from above, with a mother-of-pearl-encrusted ceiling by Buontalenti. The room's structure and decor were designed to allude to the four elements. It used to exhibit the Medici's most highly prized objects; today its best-known painting is *Angel Musician* (*c.*1520) by Fiorentina. Visitors can view but no longer access the room and some of the major works of art have been moved permanently to the Red Rooms.

The High Renaissance continues in room 19, which exhibits Perugino and Signorelli's work. These Umbrian artists worked during the 15th and 16th centuries, and the latter's tondo (circular painting) of the *Holy Family* is reputed to have inspired Michelangelo's version. Room 20 offers a break from Italian art, with works by the German painter Albrecht Dürer (1471–1528), including his *Madonna with the Pear* (1526), and by Cranach. The last few rooms on the Eastern Corridor hold works from the Venetian school in room 21; followed by Holbein and other Flemish and German Realists in room 22; and more Italian art by Mantegna and Correggio in room 23.

Michelangelo and the Florentines

Room 35 is dominated by Michelangelo's vivid *Holy Family* tondo (*c.*1506), a prelude to Mannerism produced for the wedding of Angelo Doni to Maddalena Strozzi. The room also features paintings by Fra Bartolomeo, Mariotto Albertinelli and Alfonso Berruguete. Room 28 exhibits the works of Tiziano, followed by Pamigianino in room 29. Room 35 focuses on works by Michelangelo and Florentines, whilst room 41 holds masterpieces

The Vasarian Corridor

One of the most intriguing parts of the Uffizi is the Corridoio Vasariano (closed until 2021), linking the gallery with the Palazzo Pitti on the other side of the Arno. It was built by the eponymous Vasari in 1565, so that the Medici Grand Dukes could pass between the offices at the Uffizi and their residence in the Palazzo Pitti without being seen. The passage passes over the Ponte Vecchio, through the church of Santa Felicità and on into the Pitti. The walls are hung with 17th- and 18th-century paintings and also a series of artists' self-portraits.

Fiorentina's 'Angel Musician'

by Rubens. Nearing the end, room 42 (the Niobe Room) is devoted to sculpture while room 45 (the Umbrian, Venetian and Northern European Painters Room) displays Andrea Mantegna's *Madonna of the Caves* (1488–90) as well as some superb works by German painters Albrecht Dürer and Lukas Cranach the Elder.

THE FIRST FLOOR

On the first floor are 31 rooms as well as the Verone sull'Arno, the bottom of the U-shaped corridor, which looks over the River Arno and the Piazzale degli Uffizi on the other side.

Six 'Modern Manner' Rooms house 16th-century Italian paintings – *inter alia* works by Correggio, Giorgione, Titian and Sebastiano del Piombino.

The Caravaggio Room (No 90) holds three paintings by the troubled artist, whose style is characterised by his realism and use of light (see his *Sacrifice of Isaac*, 1601–2). Caravaggio's method inspired the works by other artists contained in the same room and the next three (Nos 91–93). The last room adjacent to the Verone is the Guido Reni Room, where paintings by the 17th-century artist are displayed.

The Blue Rooms (Nos 46–55), opened in 2011, feature non-Italian art, mainly from the 17th and 18th centuries, and include portraits and self-portraits by Rembrandt. The Red Rooms (Nos 56–66) display the great Medici family portraits by Bronzino as well as works by Rosso Fiorentino, Giorgio Vasari and Andrea del Sarto. In the last room are some superb works by Raphael, including the famous *Madonna del Cardellino* (Madonna of the Goldfinch; *c.*1505) and a wistful self-portrait painted in Florence when he was only 23.

Having feasted your eyes, you are now probably ready for more solid sustenance. Two reliable places close by are **Antico Fattore**, see ❶, and **Buca dell'Orafo**, see ❷.

Food and drink

❶ ANTICO FATTORE

Via Lambertesca 1/3r; tel: 055-288 975; www.anticofattore.it; Mon–Sat noon–3pm, 7–10.30pm; €€

This long-standing trattoria close to the Uffizi offers good meat and game dishes as well as the standard Tuscan and Florentine dishes such as *trippa* (tripe) and *ribollita* (vegetable and bread soup).

❷ BUCA DELL'ORAFO

Via dei Girolami 28r; tel: 055-213 619; www.bucadellorafo.com; Tue–Sat noon–2.30pm, 7.30–10.30pm, Mon 7.30–10pm; €€

This generations-old trattoria is in the shadow of the Ponte Vecchio. It is tiny and crowded but has charm and good simple Tuscan fare, based on pasta and pulses.

The fortress-like Bargello

THE BARGELLO
AND SANTA CROCE

This walk offers a chance to visit an outstanding collection of sculpture in the Bargello. You can also eat in a chic, modern restaurant, sample some delicious ice cream and visit the tombs of Galileo, Machiavelli and Michelangelo.

DISTANCE: 800m (0.5 mile)
TIME: A full day
START: The Bargello
END: Santa Croce
POINTS TO NOTE: Begin this route mid-morning with a visit to the Bargello, then break for lunch, before carrying on to Badia Fiorentina. Note that the latter is only open to visitors on a Monday (3–6pm).

Although this tour only covers a short distance it is worth taking your time over it. Between them, the museum at the Bargello and the church of Santa Croce introduce you to many of the most famous artists and thinkers – and their works – in the history of the city.

THE BARGELLO

Start your tour outside the **Bargello ❶** (www.bargellomusei.beniculturali.it; Sun–Thu 8.15am–5pm, Fri–Sat until 7pm, closed 1st, 3rd, 5th Mon and 2nd and 4th Sun of the month) on the edge of Piazza San Firenze. This striking building with its tall, crenellated tower was built in 1255 as the city's town hall but was later used as a prison, as the names of the surrounding streets remind us: Via dei Malcontenti (Street of the Miserable) was the route taken from the Bargello to the gallows. The inner courtyard, where criminals were once executed, is now a peaceful spot, its walls studded with stones that are carved with heraldic arms.

The collections

The Bargello now contains the most important collection of sculpture in Florence, and its large holdings are worth several visits. However, those with limited time will want to concentrate on its undoubted star attractions.

The courtyard is surrounded by a cloister, which contains, among other works, Giambologna's original of *Oceanus* (1570–5) from the Boboli Garden (see page 74). Off to the right is the Sala Michelangelo, including one of the sculptor's first great works, the *Drunken Bacchus* (1496–7), who seems to be staggering off his pedestal.

Santa Croce and its piazza   *Entrance sign for Museo Nazionale*

A stately external staircase leads up to the first floor loggia where there is a lovely display of bronze birds made by Giambologna for the grotto of the Medici's Villa di Castello. On the right of the loggia is the Salone di Donatello, where you will find two of the most important works of the Renaissance: Donatello's *St George* (1416–17), commissioned by the Guild of Armourers for their niche on the exterior of Orsanmichele; and his erotically charged *David* (1440–50), who is wearing little more than an enigmatic smile. On the right-hand wall are the two trial panels made by Ghiberti and Brunelleschi, the winner and runner-up respectively in the competition of 1401 to find a designer for the Baptistry doors (see page 33); both panels depict the *Sacrifice of Isaac*.

Other highlights include the Sala del Verrocchio on the second floor, which has an excellent display of Tuscan sculpture from the 15th century, and, also on the second floor, the rooms given over to the museum's large collection of bronzes. Here you will find the model of Giambologna's *Rape of the Sabine Women,* which stands in the Loggia dei Lanzi on the Piazza della Signoria.

After taking in as many of the sculptures as you can manage, it will be time for lunch. A chic option for lunch is **Alle Murate**, see ①, just to the north of the Bargello on the right-hand side of Via dei Proconsolo.

Stained-glass window at Santa Croce

BADIA FIORENTINA

After suitable refreshment walk back down Via dei Proconsolo to the **Badia Fiorentina** ❷, the church opposite the Bargello on the corner of Via Dante Alighieri (Mon 3–6pm). The church of a Benedictine abbey, founded in 978, but considerably altered between 1627 and 1631, it merits a visit on account of a fine painting by Filippino Lippi, the *Apparition of the Virgin to St Bernard*

Galileo

Although born in Pisa, astronomer and mathematician Galileo Galilei (1564–1642) had strong ties with Florence. He first taught mathematics in the city, but after he discovered four small celestial bodies orbiting Jupiter, which he shrewdly named 'the Medicean stars', he was appointed Mathematician and Philosopher to the Grand Duke of Tuscany. He became an outspoken proponent of the Copernican system, which theorised that everything revolved around the sun. This did not sit well with the Catholic Church, which sent him into exile, first in Siena then in his villa in Arcetri, near Florence. He remained there under house arrest until his death. The city's former Museo di Storia della Scienza (Science Museum) is now the Museo Galileo (Piazza dei Giudici 1, www.museogalileo.it; daily 9.30am–6pm, Tue until 1pm), with sections devoted to the astronomer.

(1485) just inside the door.

The church's other attraction is the **Chiostro degli Aranci** (accessed to the right of the high altar), named after the orange trees that once grew here. The lovely cloister, adorned with damaged 15th-century frescoes depicting the miracles of St Bernard by Rossellino, offers excellent views of the Badia's six-sided Romanesque bell tower.

Leaving the Badia Fiorentina follow the Via della Vigna Vecchia opposite. At the second turning to the right look for the **Gelateria Vivoli**, see ❷, a well-known ice cream parlour.

SANTA CROCE

Carry on to the end of Via della Vigna Vecchia and Via de'Lavatori, then turn right into Via Guiseppe Verdi down to Piazza Santa Croce fronting the church of **Santa Croce** ❸ (www.santacroceopera.it; Mon–Sat 9.30am–5pm, Sun 2–5pm, last entry 30 mins before closing; ticket includes entrance to the Museo dell'Opera di Santa Croce and the Pazzi Chapel). This Gothic building is the burial place of many famous Florentines.

The interior
On the right of the entrance is Michelangelo's tomb, carved by Vasari; a 19th-century monument to Dante (he is buried in Ravenna); and the grave of the statesman Niccolò Machiavelli.

One of the most important monuments, however, is that of the humanist

One of the church's celebrated frescoes

Leonardo Bruni, a superb piece of Renaissance design by Rossellini in 1446–7.

The famous Cappella Bardi and Cappella Peruzzi (to the right of the high altar) are covered in frescoes depicting, in the first, the *Life of St Francis*, and the second the *Life of St John the Baptist* and *St John the Divine*. These paintings by Giotto are the best of his surviving works in Florence. The frescoes of the Cappella Baroncelli were once thought to be by Giotto, but are now attributed to his talented pupil Taddeo Gaddi. The frescoes in the Cappella Maggiore, depicting *The Legend of the True Cross*, were painted by his son Agnolo Gaddi. The corridor on the right leads past the sacristy to a chapel containing the now-empty grave of the astronomer and mathematician Galileo (see box). His body was moved to the north aisle in 1737.

Museo dell'Opera di Santa Croce

Adjoining the church is the Museo dell'Opera di Santa Croce (same opening times as the church), showcasing works including Cimabue's outstanding 13th-century *Crucifixion*, which had to be heavily restored after the 1966 floods. The museum has two serene cloisters leading to the Capella de' Pazzi, a noble building of white walls and *pietra serena* (grey sandstone) pilasters. Designed by Brunelleschi, it is considered to be one of the purest works of the Renaissance.

Having finished in Santa Croce, it may be approaching time for an *aperitivo* and something to eat. Just alongside the church, on Largo Bargellini, is **Il Francescano**, see ③.

Food and drink

① ALLE MURATE

Via del Proconsolo 16r; tel: 055-240 618; www.fishinglab.it; daily 11am–midnight; €€€€

This fine-dining restaurant occupies a palazzo with stunning frescoed vaults. Chef Giovanni Iorio has been cooking here for 30 years and his creative twist on Tuscan food, using top quality seasonal produce, is a palate-pleaser.

② GELATERIA VIVOLI

Via Isole delle Stinche 7r; tel: 055-292 334, www.vivoli.it; Apr–Oct Tue–Sat 7.30am–midnight, Sun 9am–midnight, Nov–Mar Tue–Sat 7.30am–9pm, Sun 9am–9pm; €

Despite its great reputation, this *gelateria* offers too many flavours for each to be truly world class. The chocolate ones are pretty good, though.

③ IL FRANCESCANO

Largo Bargellini 16r; tel: 055-241 605; www.trattoriailfrancescano.com; daily noon–3pm, 7pm–midnight; €€

This trattoria/pizzeria offers creative pastas, wood-fired pizzas, excellent chicken and beef dishes plus fine wines.

'Virgin and Child'

SANTA MARIA NOVELLA TO SAN MARCO

The north of the city is home to three of Florence's most important churches: Santa Maria Novella, San Lorenzo and San Marco. They are beautiful buildings in their own right, and each is full of important works of art.

DISTANCE: 3km (2 miles)
TIME: A half or a full day
START: Piazza Santa Maria Novella
END: Piazza San Marco
POINTS TO NOTE: It is only possible to do this tour in its entirety at weekends, as the church of San Marco closes at 1.50pm during the week. On weekdays, it is a half-day tour, and you could visit San Marco first thing as an add-on to tour 6, which begins in Piazza San Marco, prior to a visit to the Accademia (see page 60).

Begin the tour at **Piazza Santa Maria Novella ❶**, preferably with a relaxing breakfast or a coffee in the chic design hotel **J.K. Place**, see ❶. The vast square was used for the annual chariot race *(Palio dei Cocchi)* from the 16th to the 19th centuries: the granite obelisks at each end of the green, resting on the backs of Giambologna's *Turtles* (1608), marked the turning points on the race track.

SANTA MARIA NOVELLA

Dominating Piazza Santa Maria Novella is the monumental church, after which the square is named. Its graceful façade of green-and-white marble incorporates the name of the Rucellai family and their symbol, a billowing ship's sail, representing trade.

The Rucellai were a great Florentine family. Their name and wealth comes from *oricello*, a costly red dye from a lichen imported from the island of Mallorca. The family, who commissioned the architect Leon Battista Alberti (1404–72) to build the façade in 1470, formed a marriage alliance with the Medici; you will see that family's ring-and-ostrich-feather symbol among the complex geometric patterning.

The cemetery

You enter the church of **Santa Maria Novella ❷** (www.smn.it; Mon–Thu 9am–5.30pm, until 7pm Apr–Sept, Fri 11am–5.30pm, until 7pm Apr–Sept, Sat 9am–5.30pm, until 6.30pm July–Aug, Sun 1–5.30pm, noon–6.30pm)

One of Giambologna's turtles   *Santa Maria Novella*

through the cemetery to the right. The wall arcade surrounding the cypress-shaded grounds is carved with the coats of arms of the bankers, merchants and clothiers, whose family members are buried here.

Built in the 14th century, the cemetery is a reminder that the city was then in the grips of the Black Death. Boccaccio used the setting of this church as the springboard for his amusing *Decameron* (c.1344–50), in which a group of aristocrats escape to a villa outside Florence to avoid the disease. To entertain each other, they take turns to tell 100 tales in the 10 days referred to in the title.

The interior

The interior of the church is a breath-taking masterpiece of Gothic design, the soaring arches of the nave emphasised with alternating bands of white and grey stone. Hanging in the nave is Giotto's huge, emblematic *Crucifix*, dating to c.1290.

Another crucifixion features in Masaccio's fresco the *Trinity, Mary and St John* (1427), located in the north aisle, a landmark in the development of perspective in early Renaissance art. Behind the high altar are Ghirlandaio's colourful frescoes, the *Life of the Virgin* and *St John the Baptist* (1485–90). These repay detailed study and give

Fresh produce in the Mercato Centrale

a good idea of the living conditions of wealthy Florentines in the late 15th century. Equally compelling are Filippino Lippi's frescoes (1497–1502) in the Strozzi Chapel, to the right of the altar.

Lippi's theatrical style and love of the bizarre are well displayed in these scenes from the *Lives of St Philip* and *St John the Evangelist* (1502), which form the monumental setting for Benedetto da Maiano's tomb, built in 1486 for the wealthy banker Filippo Strozzi.

Museum and cloisters

There are more notable frescoes in the church's **cloisters,** which are included in a visit to the museum, tucked away to the left of the church façade. The **Chiostro Verde** (Green Cloister) is the most important, being the location of Uccello's dramatic *Noah and the Flood* (1450): the cloister was so named for the predominant colour of these frescoes. Damaged by the floods of 1966, they have been leached of much of their colour, but they still remain powerful and surprisingly modern in concept: Noah's Ark is not the traditional stumpy boat, but a vast, futuristic ship. The Spanish Chapel in the Dominican monastery has a fine fresco cycle by the little-known Andrea di Buonaiuto (1365-7) representing the teachings of St Thomas Aquinas.

MERCATO CENTRALE

Leave the church and turn left onto the pedestrianised Via degli Avelli. You will

soon reach Piazza dell'Unita Italiana; turn right along Via Sant'Antonino and walk down to the entrance of the huge **Mercato Centrale** ❸ (Central Market).

The stalls on the ground floor sell an abundance of meat, fish and cheese, while upstairs, under the towering glass-and-cast-iron roof, you can buy fruit, vegetables and flowers. You can also sample some Florentine specialities sold from the cooked-meat stalls or cafés downstairs; the *porchetta* (roast suckling pig) is delicious.

SAN LORENZO MARKET

We recommend you come back here for lunch, but first head south into Via dell'Ariento, where you start to pass through the huge, bustling San Lorenzo market. The stalls next to San Lorenzo church are geared to tourists and sell T-shirts, leather work and souvenirs. The deeper in you go, the more stalls you will find catering to the needs of ordinary Florentines, selling bargain-priced clothes, shoes, fabrics and table linen.

In 1990 the city administration tried to close down the market; at least, the part of it that crowds around the church. Eventually, the police gave up in the face of determined resistance from stallholders. As you walk through the market, don't neglect the little shops either side of the street, almost hidden by the stalls, where you will find all sorts of necessities for sale.

The market's imposing exterior

MEDICI CHAPELS

When you reach the Piazza San Lorenzo, right in front of you, and attached to the large bulk of the church of San Lorenzo, are the **Cappelle Medicee ❹** (Medici Chapels; www.bargellomusei.benicul turali.it; daily 8.15am–2pm, closed 1st, 3rd and 5th Mon and 2nd and 4th Sun in the month), the entrance to which is on Piazza Madonna degli Aldobrandini just to the right.

Capella dei Principi

When you first enter the chapels you will pass through the extraordinary **Cappella dei Principi** (Chapel of the Princes), the walls of which are covered in costly, multicoloured marble. The enormous sarcophagi here commemorate the 16th- and 17th-century Grand Dukes of Tuscany.

Sagrestia Nuova

From here, a corridor leads on to the **Sagrestia Nuova** (New Sacristy); though sober in contrast to the Cappelle Medicee, it contains some stupendous sculptures. The later members of the Medici family are buried here, and it was the last – and perhaps the greatest – of all Michelangelo's works for his aristocratic patrons in Florence.

The rather modest tomb of Lorenzo de'Medici is marked by Michelangelo's unfinished *Madonna and Child*. To the left is the tomb of Lorenzo's grandson, also called Lorenzo (1492–1519);

it is draped with the figures of Dawn and Dusk, while opposite is the tomb of Lorenzo's son, Giuliano. This features the awesome figures of Night and Day, symbolising the temporal and eter-

A lot of tripe

If you want to 'eat as the locals do' in Florence, then the tripe stands around San Lorenzo's Mercato Centrale (and elsewhere) will provide you with a perfect opportunity to do so – if you're game. Known as *tripperie*, these small mobile stalls sell not only tripe but just about every other part of the cow that is edible and left over after the butcher has cut up the best bits. The offal is served up either in a little dish with a plastic fork or on a *panino* or roll. Manna from heaven to the initiated, unspeakable horror to anyone else, the choice of goodies on offer varies, but you can usually find most of the following. *Trippa alla fiorentina* is traditionally stewed tripe with tomatoes and garlic, served hot with parmesan; it is also served cold as a salad. *Lampredotto* are pigs' intestines, and are usually eaten in a roll after having been simmered in a rich vegetable stock; *nervetti* are the leg tendons, again cooked in stock, while *budelline* are intestines cooked in a rich sauce. All this is normally washed down with a glass of rough-and-ready wine, often served in a plastic cup; there are no frills on tripe stands. The *tripperie* are usually open from about 9am to 7pm.

Exterior of San Lorenzo

nal forces of nature, and was carved between 1520 and 1533. Ironically, while working on them, Michelangelo was involved in the battle against the besieging forces of the Medici, to keep Florence as an independent republic. When that battle was lost, it is thought that Michelangelo hid from his patrons in this chapel. On the walls of a small room to the left of the altar are the charcoal sketches he made at this time.

LAURENTIAN LIBRARY

When you leave the Cappelle Medicee turn right along the side of the church and walk down to Piazza San Lorenzo. To the left of the front of the church is the entrance to the **Biblioteca Medicea Laurenziana** ❺ (Laurentian Library; www.bmlonline.it; Mon–Fri 9.30am–1.30pm; charge includes entrance to church), which lies at the far end of a serene cloister, from where there are unusual views of Giotto's campanile and the Duomo.

Highlights
The library, with its extraordinary vestibule and staircase, was designed by Michelangelo from 1524. His client was the Medici pope, Clement VII, and the library was built to house part of the famous collection of antique Greek and Latin manuscripts collected by Cosimo and Lorenzo de'Medici. Depending on what is currently on display, you may see Pliny the Younger's hand-writ-

ten text, a 1436 printing of Plutarch's *Moralia* (Morals) and a Greek edition (1496) of the works of the 15th-century humanist, Poliziano, with notations.

Lorenzo's staircase
The staircase that dominates the Laurentian Library's entrance vestibule was built by Bartolomeo Ammannati in 1559. Michelangelo had left Florence in 1534 before work on the library was finished, leaving only a wax model of the stairs as an indication of his wishes.

LUNCH BREAK

Before tackling the church of San Lorenzo itself, you may be ready to get something to eat. Retrace your steps a little and head back up Via dell'Ariento to Piazza del Mercato Centrale. There are some excellent places to eat in and around the market. Among them are **Nerbone**, see ❷, inside the market itself, and two *trattorie* just outside, **Mario**, see ❸, and **ZàZà**, see ❹.

SAN LORENZO

After lunch walk back down to the front of **San Lorenzo** ❻ (Mon–Sat 10am–5pm, Sun 1.30–5.30pm), which you enter through a door in the unfinished façade. In 1516, Pope Leo X commissioned Michelangelo to design San Lorenzo's façade. Michelangelo visited Carrara to select marble for the work, but the Pope then changed his mind and asked the

Fresco in San Lorenzo

artist to turn his attention to the Sagrestia Nuova in the Medici Chapels (see page 55) instead.

The interior was mainly designed by Brunelleschi and is remarkable for the elegant sobriety of the grey-and-white walls. Just before the central domed crossing are two huge marble pulpits carved by Donatello with scenes from the *Passion* and *Resurrection of Christ*. To the north of the pulpits, Bronzino's huge fresco of the *Martyrdom of St Lawrence* (1569) is unmissable. To the left, and often overlooked, is a more recent painting by Pietro Annigoni (1910–88) of the young Jesus with Joseph in a carpenter's workshop.

Famous tombs

The church was once used for state funerals, and early members of the Medici family are buried here. Cosimo, who died in 1474, is buried in a vault in front of the high altar. His father, Giovanni di Bicci de'Medici (died 1429), the wealthy banker who founded the powerful dynasty, is buried in the Sagrestia Vecchia (Old Sacristy), off the north transept, built by Brunelleschi as the family mausoleum. Donatello made the bronze entrance doors (1437–43) with their animated figures of apostles, saints, martyrs and fathers of the Church. The circular tondi (1435–43) in the chapel walls depicting the *Evangelists* and the *Life of St John the Evangelist* in terracotta and plaster relief are his too.

Giovanni's sarcophagus in the centre of the chapel is by Buggiani (1434). His grandsons, Giovanni (died 1463) and Piero de'Medici (died 1469), are buried in the huge urn-like sarcophagi of porphyry and bronze set into the walls; this was designed by Verrocchio in 1472.

MEDICI-RICCARDI PALACE

Having left the church, turn right into Via de' Gori, and back into part of the bustling San Lorenzo street market. Turn left down Via Camillo Cavour, past the Tourist Office at no. 1r, and you reach the entrance to the **Palazzo Medici-Riccardi** ❼ (www.palazzomediciriccardi.it; Thu–Tue 9am–7pm; last admission 6.30pm; entrance limited to 15 visitors every 7 minutes so be prepared to queue). This rather grim (and deliberately unostentatious) palace was built for Cosimo de'Medici between 1444 and 1464. It was from here that Cosimo and his heirs operated as unofficial rulers of Florence until Piero fled the city in 1494. The courtyard walls are studded with antique inscriptions, and the renovated **Cappella dei Magi** is home to the stunningly colourful fresco of Benozzo Gozzoli's *Journey of the Magi* (1459), in which members of the Medici family are depicted among the royal retinue.

PIAZZA SAN MARCO

Emerging from the Palazzo Medici-Riccardi, turn left and continue up

Via Cavour to **Piazza San Marco** ❽. In term time you will weave your way through chatting groups of art students who study at the Accademia, which was founded in 1563 by Vasari, with Michelangelo as one of its original members.

Now you have a choice: if you are feeling weary, you may want to finish here and head off for some refreshment. On Piazza San Marco itself is **Accademia**, see ❺, which is a good retreat, or you could try the scrumptious ice creams at **Gelateria Carabé**, see ❻. You can take your ice-cream to the delightful **Giardino dei Semplici**, also called the Orto Botanico (www.msn.unifi.it; Apr–Sept Tue–Sun 10am–6.30pm, Oct–Mar Sat–Sun 10am–4pm), on the eastern side of San Marco. Now part of the university, the garden was begun by Duke Cosimo in 1545 and was initially used to grow medicinal herbs, hence its name. Today tropical plants and Tuscan flora have been added to the collection.

If, however, it is a Saturday or Sunday, and you have the energy, then you can carry on to explore the treasures of the Museo di San Marco.

Church and Museum of San Marco

At the head of the square is the church of **San Marco** ❾ (Mon–Sat 9.45am–4.45pm, Sun 2–5pm), which was remodelled by Michelozzo from 1437 onwards. The interior is decorative, but of more interest are the peaceful cloisters and monastic buildings attached to it that make up the fascinating **Museo di San Marco** ❿ (www.museumsinflo rence.com; Mon–Fri 8.15am–1.50pm, Sat–Sun 8.15am–4.50pm, closed 1st, 3rd and 5th Sun and 2nd and 4th Mon in the month).

Many famous names are connected with San Marco. Cosimo de' Medici paid for the building of this monastery, which was originally (from 1436) occupied by Dominican friars from the nearby hill town of Fiesole. Fra Angelico spent most of his life within its walls, and the museum contains many of his paintings; his *Crucifixion* (1442) is in the Chapter House.

The Dormitory

The **Dormitorio** is the high point of the museum, consisting of 44 monastic cells under a great open roof. Fra Angelico's *Annunciation* is located at the top of the stairs. Beyond, each cell contains a small fresco that is stripped to its essential religious significance; they were intended as aids to contemplation. The frescoes in cells 1 to 10, on the left, are probably the work of Fra Angelico; the rest are by his assistants. In cell 7, the *Mocking of Christ* is typical of his style, where disembodied hands beat Christ about the head. Savonarola (see page 39) believed in the futility of earthly deeds and passions and saw only the afterlife as important, so, fittingly, cells 12 to 14 contain his hair shirt, as well as a copy of a contemporary painting of his execution.

The other wing of the Dormitory leads past the **Biblioteca** (Library), a graceful

Nuns and priest taking a stroll

hall built to house the illuminated manuscripts donated by Cosimo de'Medici to create Europe's first public library, and designed by Michelozzo in 1441. The cells that Cosimo reserved for his own retreats (nos 38 and 39) are at the end of the corridor. The wall of cell 39 is decorated with the *Three Kings and their retinue visiting the Nativity*, in a scene painted by Benozzo Gozzoli.

Food and drink

1 J.K. PLACE
Piazza Santa Maria Novella 7; tel: 055-264 5181; www.jkplace.com; 11am–11pm (breakfast 7–11am); €€€€
In this plush design hotel with the atmosphere of a private house you can order a drink (the cocktails are particularly good), a coffee and light snacks or a meal from anywhere in the building including the bar. There is a lovely lounge space with a large fireplace as well as a romantic rooftop terrace.

2 NERBONE
Piazza del Mercato Centrale, inside the market; tel: 055-219 949; Mon–Sat 8am–3pm; €
One of the most popular lunch spots of the area, Nerbone serves up local dishes, such as *tripa alla fiorentina* (tripe in a tomato sauce), with seasonal ingredients on a daily menu. The *panino con bollito* (boiled beef sandwich) is a favourite.

3 MARIO
Via Rosina 2r; tel: 055-218 550; www. trattoria-mario.com; Mon–Sat noon– 3.30pm; €
Hidden away behind market stalls, this *trattoria* boasts a lively atmosphere and is popular with the local stallholders. Try the typical *ribollita* (vegetable and bread soup).

4 TRATTORIA ZÀZÀ
Piazza del Mercato Centrale 26r; tel: 055-215 411; www.trattoriazaza.it; daily 11am–11pm; €€€
Set in the piazza behind the market, this lively, rustic *trattoria* offers a range of meat and fish-based dishes, along with excellent pizzas and a good choice of wines.

5 ACCADEMIA
Piazza San Marco 7r; tel: 055-217 343; www.ristoranteaccademia.it; daily noon– 2.30pm and 7–10.30pm; €€
Opposite the front of the church of San Marco, this restaurant is both a haven from cultural overload and a convivial setting where pizzas, pasta and other food are washed down with the good house wine.

6 GELATERIA CARABÉ
Via Ricasoli 60r; tel: 055-289 476; www. parcocarabe.it; Tue–Sun 11am–7pm; €
This place is not to be missed if you are a fan of ice cream. Sicilian *gelati* are made from ingredients shipped in from the island itself.

Sculpted torso, Accademia

THE ACCADEMIA TO THE MUSEO ARCHEOLOGICO

This route takes you from the collection of Michelangelo's sculpture in the Accademia, via the beautiful square of Santissima Annunziata with its Brunelleschi buildings, to the superb Archaeological Museum.

DISTANCE: 300m (0.25 mile)
TIME: A full day
START: Galleria dell'Accademia
END: Museo Archeologico
POINTS TO NOTE: This walk starts where route 5 ends, on Piazza San Marco. On a weekday, when the Museo di San Marco closes early (see page 58), it would be possible to join the two routes together, starting here with the museum before moving on to the Accademia. However, to try and combine the two routes in total would be far too long for a single day's sightseeing.

This short route packs a lot into a small geographical area. The highlight for many will be a sight of the restored original of Michelangelo's *David* in the Galleria dell'Accademia, as opposed to the copy in front of the Palazzo Vecchio.

THE ACCADEMIA

Start the route at Piazza San Marco, on the far side of which, at Via Ricasoli

58, is the **Galleria dell' Accademia ❶** (www.galleriaaccademiafirenze.beni culturali.it; Tue–Sun 8.15am–6.50pm). This gallery attracts a huge number of visitors, and long queues can build up, especially at Easter and in the summer. If you find a queue has already formed, don't despair – it moves quite quickly. There is no café in the museum itself, but if you are in need of refreshment before going in head for **Robiglio**, see ❶, on Via dei Servi close to Piazza Santissima.

The collection
The Accademia's collection contains sculpture and early Renaissance religious art, and has been expanded to include a display of musical instruments. On entry, the Sala del Colosso showcases the plaster cast of Giambologna's *Rape of the Sabine Women* (on display in the Loggia dei Lanzi, see page 38) and a collection of colourful religious art from the early Cinquecento (16th century).

The door located to the left of the entrance takes you into the gallery proper,

Exterior of the Accademia   *Spedale degli Innocenti detail*

starting with the **Galleria dei Prigionieri**, where Michelangelo's fine unfinished *Four Slaves* (c.1530), originally intended for the tomb of Pope Julius II, are displayed. The view from here of *David* (see page 62), in the domed **Tribuna di Michelangelo**, is absolutely stunning.

Off to the left of the Tribuna di Michelangelo are three small rooms – the **Sala del Duecento e Prima Trecento**, the **Sala di Giotto e della sua scuola** and the **Sala di Giovanni da Milano e degli Orcagna**. These all hold early Florentine works, some by Gaddi and

Daddi. The *Tree of Life* (c.1310) by Buonaguida is a highlight. At the end of the hall the Salone dell'Ottocento is packed with plaster busts and statues once used by Accademia students.

Stairs lead to the first floor and four further rooms. The first two exhibit attractive work from the late 14th century. The following room is dedicated to Florentine painter Lorenzo Monaco, whose work expresses the bridge between Gothic and Renaissance art, which is the key to understanding the Florentine style.

The Medici coat of arms inside the Hospital

Back downstairs, adjoining the lobby, the **Sala del Colosseo** displays the full-size plaster model of Giambologna's *Rape of the Sabine Women*, the marble version of which stands in the Loggia of the Palazzo Vecchio.

David

Michelangelo's *David* was sculpted between 1501 and 1504, and, through its depiction of the young boy who slew Goliath, it symbolises the birth of republican Florence. Originally situated in front of the Palazzo Vecchio (a copy stands in situ), the statue, which stands at over 4m (13ft), was moved to the Accademia in 1873 for reasons of preservation; a decision that was heavily criticised at the time. The marble from which *David* was carved was famously rejected as faulty by other artists, but the then 29-year-old Michelangelo sought to embrace its faults and patches of discoloration. *David* is celebrated for being of perfect proportions when viewed from below and is hailed as a testament to Michelangelo's eye for detail: just see the muscle contour of the legs and the veins in the arms (even more apparent since the controversial clean up in 2004), which can be admired from every angle thanks to the way the statue is displayed. The eyes are of particular interest for their heart-shaped pupils.

From here a short hallway brings you to the **Dipartimento degli Srumentali Musicali**, with musical instruments from the 17th to 19th centuries. Highlights are a Stradivari violin, a cello by Amati and the world's oldest surviving upright piano.

HOSPITAL OF THE INNOCENTS

Turn right out of the Accademia and then right again into Via Cesare Battisti. This leads to the pedestrianised **Piazza della Santissima Annunziata ❷**, one of the most beautiful squares in Florence. In the centre of the square is an equestrian statue of *Duke Ferdinand I*, by Giambologna; this is partnered by two bronze fountains (by Pietro Tacca, 1608) featuring rather strange-looking marine monsters.

On the southeast side of the square is the gracious colonnade of the **Spedale degli Innocenti ❸**, started by Brunelleschi in 1419 and the first classical loggia of its type. Here the columns of *pietra serena* (grey sandstone) alternate with Luca della Robbia's blue-and-white terracotta roundels that depict a baby in swaddling clothes – the symbol of the Innocenti orphanage located just behind. The orphanage, opened in 1444 and the first in the world, is still used for its original purpose.

The building also houses the **Innocenti Museum** and the **Galleria dello Spedale degli Innocenti** (www.istitu

The grand, neoclassical Museo Archeologico

todeglinnocenti.it; daily 10am–7pm), a gallery of pictures donated by patrons, including Ghirlandaio's *Adoration of the Magi* (1488). Brunelleschi's portico was copied on the opposite side of the square, where it now fronts a fine hotel, the Loggiato dei Serviti.

SANTISSIMA ANNUNZIATA

On the north side of the square is the grand entrance to the church of **Santissima Annunziata** ❹ (daily 7.30am–12.30pm, 4–6.30pm). This contains some fine frescoes, such as Andrea del Sarto's *Birth of the Virgin* (1514) and, in the adjacent Chiostro dei Morti (Cloister of the Dead), his *Holy Family*.

ARCHEOLOGICAL MUSEUM

Turn left out of the church and cross the road for the **Museo Archeologico** ❺ (Piazza Santissima Annunziata 9b; Sat–Sun 8.30am–2pm, Tue–Fri 8.30am–7pm).

The first floor is partly given over to the exceptional Etruscan collections and temporary exhibitions. The tomb sculpture gives a touching insight into the everyday lives of these peaceful people. The real stars of the museum, however, are the Etruscan bronzes. The 5th-century BC *Chimera*, part-lion, part-goat and part-snake, was discovered in Arezzo in 1554 and greatly admired by Renaissance bronze-cast-

ers, including Benvenuto Cellini, who was entrusted with the restoration of a broken foreleg. The *Arringatore* (2nd century BC) was discovered in Trasimeno in 1556.

Also on the first floor are Egyptian treasures while the revamped second floor is dedicated to ancient Greek, Etruscan and Roman art.

Options for eating are fairly limited in the immediate vicinity. We recommend heading south down Via dei Fibbai and then right into Via degli Alfani for **Lo Skipper**, see ②.

Food and drink

❶ ROBIGLIO
Via dei Servi 112; tel: 055-212 784; www.robigliocatering.com; daily 7.30am–10pm; €

This is one of the chain of Robiglio cafés serving delicious pastries and chocolates as well as tasty lunches. Do try the squidgy choux buns.

❷ LO SKIPPER
Via degli Alfani 78; tel: 055-284 019; www.ristoranteskipper.firenze.it; Mon–Fri noon–3pm and 8pm–midnight, Sat 8pm–midnight; €€

With a concentration on fish dishes, this restaurant, run by a nautical club, offers good Italian food as well as dishes inspired by other culinary traditions, such as Mexican and Greek.

Piazza della Repubblica

AROUND PIAZZA DELLA REPUBBLICA

The roads to the west of Florence's grand 19th-century Piazza della Repubblica are home to many of the city's designer shops, including famous Florentine names such as Gucci, Pucci and Ferragamo.

DISTANCE: 1km (0.5 mile)
TIME: A half day
START: Piazza della Repubblica
END: Mercato Nuovo
POINTS TO NOTE: This route is best done in the morning, if you want to visit the Palazzo Davanzati. Book ahead for the Ferragamo Shoe Museum.

Begin the route at the large open square of **Piazza della Repubblica ❶**.

PIAZZA DELLA REPUBBLICA

Built on the site of the Roman forum, this square formed the centrepiece of the 19th-century rebuilding project that sought to transform Florence into a capital fit for the new United Kingdom of Italy. As it turned out, the city was only the capital between 1865 and 1871, and the redevelopment of the old ghetto was halted by the outcry from foreign aficionados of the narrow streets and medieval archi-

tecture. All that remains of the grand plan is the piazza, and the grand triumphal arch bearing an inscription to the effect that 'the ancient heart of the city was restored to new life from its former squalor in 1895'.

The square and its immediate surroundings form a pleasant contrast to the sometimes rather stark streets of the old city. More importantly, it is also home to some swish cafés, in which you can have a coffee before starting your walk. The three most famous are the **Giubbe Rosse**, see ❶, **Gilli**, see ❷, and **Paszkowski**, see ❸.

STROZZI PALACE

Once fortified, take the western exit from the square along Via degli Strozzi. At the second turning on the left is Piazza Strozzi, location of the imposing **Palazzo Strozzi ❷** (www.palazzostrozzi.org; open during exhibitions daily 10am–8pm, Thu until 11pm). This was the last, and largest, of the Renaissance palaces built in the city. Constructed by the banker Fil-

Expect to pass some fine shoe shops

ippo Strozzi between 1489 and 1536, the building of what was an even bigger palace than the Medici's Palazzo Medici-Riccardi (see page 57) bankrupted the family. The façade has a huge classical cornice, and the massive stone walls have Renaissance torch holders and lamp brackets. The interior courtyard was greatly remodelled in the 19th century and is relatively charmless, but it has a café and a small museum that shows how the palace once looked. The palace is now used to hold major exhibitions and also contains the Gabinetto Vieusseux public library.

VIA DE' TORNABUONI

At the end of Via degli Strozzi turn left into **Via de' Tornabuoni ❸**, Florence's most upmarket shopping street. Palaces here house the showrooms of Pucci, Ferragamo, Armani, Prada, Valentino, Versace and La Perla. Florence has long been known for its fabrics, leather and superb craftsmanship, which helped it to become fabulously wealthy during the Renaissance.

Santa Trinità

At the end of Via de' Tornabuoni is busy Piazza Santa Trinità and, on the right,

Sala dei Papagalli in Palazzo Davanzati

the church of **Santa Trinità** ❹ (daily 7am–noon and 4–7pm). Here, the relative austerity of the 13th-century Gothic interior contrasts with the Baroque façade and Ghirlandaio's stunningly colourful frescoes and altarpiece of the Sassetti Chapel, to the right of the choir. The frescoes (1483) illustrate the *Life of St Francis*, and the altarpiece (1485) shows the *Nativity*. Other frescoes depict scenes from Classical literature and mythology, set against a Florentine backdrop.

Ferragamo Museum

Opposite the church is the **Palazzo Spini Feroni** ❺, one of the city's few remaining 13th-century palaces. Its ground floor is now home to the flagship store of Salvatore Ferragamo. The famous shoe designer used to live in the palace and the excellent **Museo Ferragamo** (www.ferragamo.com; daily 10am–7.30pm) has an exhibition on his life and work, as well as some spectacular shoes.

DAVANZATI PALACE

Now take Via Porta Rossa, behind the Palazzo Spini Feroni, to the **Palazzo Davanzati** ❻ (tel: 055-238 8610; www.bargellomusei.beniculturali.it; Mon–Fri 8.15am–2pm, Sat–Sun 1.15–7pm, closed 2nd and 4th Sun and 1st, 3rd and 5th Mon in the month; the two upper floors are visited in guided groups by appointment only). The façade dates from the mid-14th century and is typical of Tuscan pre-Renaissance architecture, including features such as the so-called depressed arch over the doors and windows. The coat of arms is that of the Davanzati family, who owned the palace from 1518 until 1538. The open loggia that crowns the palace was added in the 16th century. Now restored the house gives a fascinating insight into life in medieval Florence.

Highlights

Inside are a beautiful courtyard and an elegant stone staircase supported by flying arches. Note the well to the right of the entrance with a pulley system enabling buckets of water to be lifted to each of the five floors – a private water supply was a considerable luxury.

The principal living rooms occupy the first floor, the *piano nobile*, where you will find the gorgeously frescoed dining

---

Il Porcellino

Located south of the Mercato Nuovo, Il Porcellino attracts countless visitors who come to rub the snout of this bronze boar that was copied from the Roman statue in the Uffizi, itself a copy of an Hellenic original. The statue you see today is actually yet another copy; its predecessor was sent for restoration in 1998. It is said that anyone who rubs the snout is certain to return to the city. Coins dropped in the trough below are distributed to city charities.

Leather goods at the Mercato Nuovo

room, the **Sala dei Papagalli** (Room of the Parrots) after the birds pictured in the borders.

The bedchambers on the floors above also have murals, notably the one decorated with scenes from the 13th-century French romance, the *Châtelaine de Vergy*. Although the furnishings in each room – beds, chests and stools – may look sparse, they represent a considerable degree of luxury for the time, as do the private bathrooms off each room, complete with toilets and terracotta waste pipes. In the kitchen situated on the top floor you will find an array of contemporary utensils, including equipment for kneading and shaping pasta.

MERCATO NUOVO

At the end of Via Porta Rossa, on the right, is the **Mercato Nuovo ❼** (New Market). A market has existed here since the 11th century, and the 'new' current arcade was built between 1547 and 1551 for the sale of silk and gold. Later it gained the name 'straw market' (Mercato della Paglia) from the woven-straw *(raffia)* goods sold there by peasants. Leather goods and T-shirts now form the bulk of the offerings.

For something to eat, if you do not fancy the tripe stand in the southwest corner of the arcade, you can always return to the cafés on Piazza della Repubblica or head a little further east to Via dei Tavolini to the **Cantinetta dei Verrazzano**, see ❹, for some tasty nibbles.

Food and drink

❶ GIUBBE ROSSE
Piazza della Repubblica 13/14r; tel: 055-212 280; www.giubberosse.it; daily 8am–11pm; €€€€
Florence's famous literary café is more touristy now. It offers panini and a lunch buffet or an upmarket dinner menu.

❷ GILLI
Piazza della Repubblica 36–39; tel: 055-213 896; www.gilli.it; daily 7.30am–1am; €€€
This elegant place claims to be Florence's oldest café. It is also a luxurious *chocolaterie*.

❸ PASZKOWSKI
Piazza della Repubblica 31–35r; tel: 055-210 236; www.caffepaszkowski.it; daily 7am–2am; €€€
This grand café is great for coffee and cake, lunch, or after-dinner drinks accompanied by live music.

❹ CANTINETTA DEI VERRAZZANO
Via dei Tavolini 18r; tel: 055-268 590; www.verrazzano.com; Mon–Sat 8am–4.30pm, Sun 10am–5pm; €
This is part bakery, part *enoteca*. The bakery has special flavoured breads and pastries. Sit in the *enoteca* for a glass of Chianti and some *pecorino* cheese with balsamic vinegar, or focaccia with prosciutto.

Local artisan shopkeeper

OLTRARNO

On the south side of the Arno is the laid-back district of Oltrarno, where a wealth of sights, including the stunning frescoes in the Brancacci Chapel, as well as some lovely restaurants and bars, can be found.

DISTANCE: 1.5km (1 mile)
TIME: A half day
START: Santa Felicità
END: Porta San Frediano
POINTS TO NOTE: If you wanted to make a full day of this route, then it could be combined with a visit to the Palazzo Pitti and Boboli Garden (route 9) by adding these sights from the Piazza de'Pitti. Bear in mind, though, that this would make for a lot of sightseeing.

Oltrarno literally means 'beyond the Arno', and this route takes in some of the most important sights in the neighbourhoods on the southern bank of Florence's river. First brought inside the city walls in the 14th century, this area still feels a little separate from the rest of Florence.

SANTA FELICITÀ

Begin on the southern side of the Ponte Vecchio. Before you start it might be worth popping along to Piazza dei Rossi

(at the far end of Piazza Santa Felicità), where you can get a drink and something to eat at the lovely *enoteca* **Le Volpi e l'Uva**, see ①.

From the bridge, walk down Via de'Guicciardini to the church of **Santa Felicità ❶** (Mon–Sat 9.30am–12.30pm and 3.30–5.30pm), on the left. Take a look inside this church, which has two remarkable works by the Mannerist artist, Pontormo, an *Annunciation* and a *Deposition* (both 1525–8). Their colours are almost acidic in their vividness and a contrast to the more subdued hues used by Renaissance painters.

Turn left out of the church and walk down to the Piazza de'Pitti. Dominating the square is the huge Palazzo Pitti. This, and the Boboli Garden just behind, are explored in route 9 (see page 72).

CASA GUIDI

On the far (southern) corner of Piazza de'Pitti look out for the first-floor **Casa Guidi ❷** (Guidi House; tel: 055-354 457; Apr–Nov Mon, Wed and Fri

View towards Oltrarno

3–6pm; donations welcome), at Piazza San Felice 8. It is located inside the 15th-century Palazzo Guidi, where the poets Robert and Elizabeth Browning lived from 1847 (shortly after their secret marriage) until Elizabeth's death in 1861. It was Elizabeth who called the apartment 'Casa Guidi' to change 'a mere palace into a home'. It is also available to rent via the Landmark Trust (www.landmarktrust.org.uk).

PIAZZA SANTO SPIRITO

From here, turn into Via Mazzetta, which leads into Piazza Santo Spirito where there is a small market each morning from Monday to Saturday. The square is a good place to get something to eat, and two places worth trying are the **Osteria Santo Spirito**, see ❷, and **Borgo Antico**, see ❸.

There are many good antiques shops nearby, especially around Via Maggio. This part of the city is very different from the historic centre – bustling, lively and authentically Florentine.

Santo Spirito

At the head of the square is the church of **Santo Spirito** ❸ (Mon–Tue and Thu–Fri 10am–noon and 4pm–6pm, Wed and

Pretty backstreet

Sat 10am–noon). Begun in 1436, it was regarded as Brunelleschi's masterpiece and is a superb example of Renaissance Classicism. Among the works of art on display in the church, note Filippino Lippi's *Madonna and Saints* (*c.*1490), in the right-hand transept.

Adjacent is the **Cenacolo di Santo Spirito** (Mon–Sat 10am–5pm, Sun 1–5pm), the refectory, which contains Orcagna's 14th-century fresco *The Last Supper*. Although the work was damaged in the 18th century, the outer part can still be seen. Above it is a more complete *Crucifixion*.

BRANCACCI CHAPEL

Walk back to the piazza, turn right into Via Sant'Agostino and continue down Via Santa Monaca to reach Piazza del Carmine. The church of **Santa Maria del Carmine ❹** was destroyed by fire in 1771, and subsequently rebuilt. However

Masaccio

Born Tomasso Cassai (1401–78), Masaccio is credited with the invention of scientific perspective, whereby lines of sight in a painting disappear towards a single point of reference. This enabled him to give his works a greater realism than those of earlier painters. Another of his innovations was the lighting of a picture from a single source, so creating a more realistic chiaroscuro (interplay of light and shade).

the **Cappella Brancacci ❺** (tel: 055-276 8224; Mon, Wed–Sat 10am–5pm, Sun 1–5pm), just to the right, was spared. A maximum of 30 visitors are allowed in at one time for only 30 minutes and reservations are necessary. The ticket includes a 40-minute film in English.

Once inside this tiny chapel you are brought face to face with the restored frescoes on the *Life of St Peter*, begun by Masolino, continued by Masaccio from 1425 until his death in 1428, and completed by Filippino Lippi in 1480. Masaccio's contribution has been hailed as a superb example of the emerging Renaissance style, remarkable for his use of perspective and chiaroscuro to highlight the central figures. A serene St Peter moves among the poor and crippled, distributing alms and working miracles, against the backdrop of 15th-century Florence.

Masaccio's work is mainly in the upper tier of the fresco and includes his *Expulsion from Paradise*, in which the figures of Adam and Eve, no longer beautiful as in Masolino's *Temptation* scene opposite, are racked with misery. The scenes in the lower tier, mostly by Filippino Lippi, are equally distinguished.

SAN FREDIANO

Across the expansive Piazza del Carmine, spoilt by its use as a car park, lies Borgo San Frediano. This is the principal street of a characterful, traditionally

San Frediano

working-class, district. A little way down is the church of **San Frediano** ⑥ (Mon–Sat 9.30–11.30am and 4.30–5.30pm, Sun 10–11.30am, 5–6pm). It has an unfinished rough stone façade but possesses one of the finest Baroque interiors in Florence. The frescoed dome over the main altar is by Antonio Domenico Gabbiani. Also notable are the 14th-century *Madonna of the Smile*

and, in the refectory, Bernardino Poccetti's *Last Supper* (*c.*1600).

At the western end of the Borgo is **Porta San Frediano** ⑦, built in 1324 it is one of the best-preserved stretches of the 14th-century city walls.

This part of the city has quite a number of decent places to eat, and at the end of your route you could head for **Dolce Vita**, see ④ or **Napoleone**, see ⑤.

Food and drink

① LE VOLPI E L'UVA

Piazza dei Rossi 1; tel: 055-239 8132; www.levolpieluva.com; Mon–Sat 11am–9pm; €

This superb little wine bar has a fabulous selection of Italian wines, including little-known vintages from small producers. They also serve tasty plates of cheese and *salumi*, as well as *schiacciatine* (thin flat bread) and hot focaccia topped with mushrooms and prosciutto.

② OSTERIA SANTO SPIRITO

Piazza Santo Spirito 16r; tel: 055-238 2383; www.osteriasantospirito.it; daily noon–11.30pm; €€€

A somewhat trendy hang-out with colourful decor and noisy music. The food is inventive, and fish figures largely. Be sure to order some of the excellent pasta on offer; the *orecchiette* is recommended.

③ BORGO ANTICO

Piazza Santo Spirito 6r; tel: 055-210 437;

www.borgoanticofirenze.com; daily noon–midnight; €€

A cosy restaurant with a standard menu and an extensive range of daily specials. Try the ravioli for a rich, filling pasta dish, or one of the *secondi* from the specials menu.

④ DOLCE VITA

Piazza del Carmine 6/r; tel: 055-284 595; http://new.dolcevitafirenze.it; daily 8pm–2am, *aperitivo* daily 7.30–9.30pm; €€

This trendy, often busy bar, with cool interiors and live music (Wed–Thu), is beloved by Florentine students, who come here for the *aperitivo* and its great cocktails.

⑤ NAPOLEONE

Piazza del Carmine 24; tel: 055-260 8414; www.trattorianapoleone.it; Sun–Thu 6–11.30pm, Fri–Sat 6pm–midnight; €€

This colourful *trattoria*, with a quirky but modern interior, is set in a quiet location near the church. It serves decent traditional Tuscan dishes such as steaks, salads and plates of *salumi*.

Boboli Garden views

THE PITTI PALACE
AND BOBOLI GARDEN

*Taken over by the Medici when its owner went bust, the huge Pitti
Palace is now home to some exceptional works of art, but perhaps its
jewel in the crown is the lovely Boboli Garden.*

DISTANCE: 1km (0.5 mile)
TIME: A full day
START: Pitti Palace
END: Boboli Garden
POINTS TO NOTE: It might be possible
to fit this route in with the general
Oltrarno walk (route 8) but it would mean
rushing around the Palatine Gallery and
gardens, as well as missing out on the
other museums in the palace.

It is easy to spend a full day, or more,
over this route. As well as a stunning
collection of art, there are museums of
fashion, porcelain and silver, as well as
the beautiful Boboli Garden – one of the
highlights of a trip to Florence.

PITTI PALACE

The route begins on Piazza de'Pitti, in
front of the imposing, and somewhat
austere, façade of the **Palazzo Pitti ❶**.

The palace was begun in the late
1450s for the banker Luca Pitti, but the
cost of the building brought him to the

verge of bankruptcy, and, after his death,
his heirs sold it to Eleonora di Toledo, the
Spanish-born wife of Duke Cosimo I, in
1549. The Medici family moved here in
1550, and from then on it served as the
home of Tuscany's rulers, gradually being
expanded to its present immense bulk.

PALATINE GALLERY

Start in the left wing of the first floor of the
palace, home to the **Galleria Palatina**
(www.uffizi.it/palazzo-pitti/galleria-
palatina; Tue–Sun 8.15am–6.50pm).
This gallery contains some outstanding
works of art hung in beautiful rooms. The
ticket office is in the right wing, and the
entrance to the gallery is off the internal
courtyard.

The gallery begins with a series of
antechambers containing some notable
paintings. Filippo Lippi's beautiful tondo
of the *Madonna and Child* and Rubens'
Three Graces hang in the Sala di Pro-
meteo (room 14) and the Sala dei Putti
respectively. The Sala di Bagno (Bathroom), decorated with stucco nymphs
and four marble Nereides, was designed

Pitti Palace

for the French Emperor Napoleon, after he had conquered northern Italy.

Mythological decoration

The most splendid apartments overlook the main piazza. The regal setting of these six rooms is matched by masterpieces on the walls by Raphael, Rubens and Titian. The Sala dell' Illiade (room 27) is one of the most sumptuous in the palace, with a frescoed neoclassical ceiling inspired by Homeric myths. The splendid Sala di Saturno (room 28) is wall-to-wall with masterpieces, including some of Raphael's finest works; it also has a fine 17th-century ceiling, depicting an Olympian scene in gilt and stuccowork.

The adjoining Sala di Giove (room 29) has the grandeur befitting a Medici throne room and is decorated with Pietro da Cortona's frescoes glorifying the young Prince Ferdinando. The ceiling is supported by a seething mass of nymphs, gods and entwined cherubs, while the far door is framed by masterpieces painted by Raphael *(Woman with a Veil)*, and Giorgione. Next, the Sala di Marte (Room 30) contains an array of Flemish and Italian masterpieces, set against vibrant red damask walls, including Rubens' great martial work, *The Consequences of War* (1637).

The Sala di Apollo (room 31), which is frescoed and dotted with statuary, is equally ornate. Framing the entrance doorway are masterpieces by Titian, such as his luminous *Mary Magdalene*, a nude wreathed in the artist's trademark Titian hair.

The Sala di Venere (room 32) is named after Canova's *Venus Italica* (c.1812), commissioned by Napoleon as a replacement for the Hellenistic *Venus de' Medici* that he had spirited away to Paris. Canova's masterpiece of neoclassical statuary is the companion piece to the *Venus*, which is now in the Uffizi (see page 44).

Royal apartments

On the first floor in the right wing, beyond the Galleria Palatina, are the **Appartamento Reali**

Statues dot the garden

(Royal Apartments). Only some of these rooms are open at any one time. These are rather ostentatious rooms, with plush and heavy carpets and draped fabrics. Several are named after the colour in which they are decorated, and contain paintings and portraits; there are also the Queen's Apartments, the King's Apartments and a ceremonial room, all filled with exquisite furniture.

NICHE MUSEUMS

In addition to the Galleria Palatina there are four other museums in the Palazzo Pitti (www.uffizi.it/en/pitti-palace). A cumulative ticket is available for all four.

Decorative Arts Museum
Located on the ground floor, the **Museo degli Argenti** (Silver Museum; Tue–Sun 8.15am–6.50pm, last entrance 30 minutes before closure) is in the left-hand corner of the courtyard, while the **Museo delle Porcellane** (Porcelain Museum; daily Nov–Feb 8.15am–4.30pm, Mar 8.15am–5.30pm, Apr–May and Sept–Oct 8.15am–6.30pm, Jun–Aug 8.15am–6.50pm; closed first and last Mon of the month, last entry 60 minutes before closure; same ticket as the Museo degli Argenti) is situated in the Boboli Garden. The former contains silver and other baubles collected by the Medicis; the latter some fine porcelain.

Modern Art and Costume Galleries
The second floor houses the **Galleria d'Arte Moderna** (same times and ticket as the Galleria Palatina), which contains mainly neoclassical and Romantic and Impressionist Italian works of art.

Also on the second floor is the **Galleria del Costume** (same times and ticket as the Museo degli Argenti), whose 6,000-piece holding of clothing, theatrical costumes and accessories are supplemented by special exhibitions.

BOBOLI GARDEN

Just behind the palace is the formal **Giardino di Boboli** ❷ (daily Nov–Feb 8.15am–4.30pm, Mar 8.15am–5.30pm, Apr–May and Sept–Oct 8.15am–6.30pm, Jun–Aug 8.15am–6.50pm; closed first and last Mon of the month, last entry 60 minutes before closure; same ticket as Museo degli Argenti). In 2013, the garden became a Unesco World Heritage Site, together with another park, Pratolino Park-Villa Demidoff, and 12 Medici villas. The Boboli Garden is entered from the inner courtyard via a flight of steps that leads to a terrace to the rear of the palace in front of Susini's fountain, constructed in 1641. The fountain sits at the focal point of a grassy amphitheatre, laid out from 1630 to 1635.

Statuary, structures and stonework
The huge granite basin nearby is from Rome's ancient Caracalla baths. A series of terraces leads up to Stoldo Lorenzi's *Neptune Fountain* (Fontana di Nettuno;

Relaxing in the sunshine

1565–9) and to the left is the Baroque **Kaffeehaus**, built in 1776 as a spot from which Duke Leopold's court could appreciate the views of Florence.

Heading back to the gardens, a path leads up to the statue of Abundance (*Abbondanza*), then to the enclosed **Giardino del Cavaliere**, constructed in 1529 and now restored with low box hedges, rose bushes and lovely views.

Walk past the gardeners' houses until you reach the top of the **Viottolone**, a shady, cypress avenue planted in 1637. This is a magical spot.

Buontalenti Grotto

From the top of the Viottolone, a path takes you back to the east wing of the Pitti Palace via the smaller Palazzina della Meridiana and past the **Grotta di Buontalenti** (only with a guide, daily 11am, 1pm, 3pm, Apr–Sept: also 4pm and 5pm), a fantastic grotto with copies of Michelangelo's *Four Slaves* set in the four corners. Further inside, you will come across *Paris seducing Helen of Troy* in Vincenzo de'Rossi's erotic sculpture, and, almost out of sight at the rear of the cave, is Giambologna's *Venus* emerging from her bath.

GIARDINO BARDINI

The **Bardini Gardens** (Via dei Bardi 1 and Costa San Giorgio 2; www.bardinipeyron. it; same times and ticket as Giardino di Boboli except Jun–Aug until 7.30pm) rise up in terraces towards Piazzale Michelan-gelo. More peaceful than the Boboli Gardens they feature statues, fountains and fine views over Florence. The **Villa Bardini** (Tue–Sun 10am–7pm) features a small museum with some extravagant creations by fashion designer Roberto Capucci. The gardens can also be accessed from Via dei Bardi, Piazza dei Mozzi, near the Museo Bardini (see page 76).

For a restorative meal with a truffle theme head for the **Caffè Pitti**, see ❶, opposite the palace on Piazza de' Pitti; or, close by, the **Pitti Gola e Cantina** see ❷ is a great place for a glass of wine and tasty Tuscan fare.

Food and drink

❶ CAFFÈ PITTI

Piazza de'Pitti 9; tel: 055-239 9863; www. caffepitti.it; daily noon–11pm; €€
This venue located directly opposite the Palazzo Pitti is a popular hang-out for locals and tourists alike. Truffles are a speciality of the house, served with pasta or tenderloin steak. Truffle tastings take place here in November and December.

❷ PITTI GOLA E CANTINA

Piazza de'Pitti 16; tel: 055-212 704; www.pittigolaecantina.com; Wed–Mon noon–11pm; €
Lined with shelving filled with bottles of wine, many available by the glass, this is a great little *enoteca*. To try the wine tasting dinner make sure to book ahead.

The view from Piazzale Michelangelo

SAN MINIATO AL MONTE

The fairly strenuous walk to the jewel-like church of San Miniato and the Piazzale Michelangelo is amply rewarded by sweeping views. Then meander down, passing villas and fields, to the Belvedere Fortress.

DISTANCE: 5km (3 miles)
TIME: A full day
START: Ponte alle Grazie
END: Via de'Bardi
POINTS TO NOTE: This route requires quite a bit of walking, some of it uphill, so it is best to devote a whole day to it and to take things quite slowly and stop and eat en route. Note the Museo Stefano Bardini is only open Fri–Mon.

The lovely Romanesque church of San Miniato al Monte sits on a hill to the south of the city. The walk up to the church takes in Piazzale Michelangelo, justly famous for its views over Florence. On the way down, take in the Belvedere, a huge fortress now used for exhibitions.

Begin on the southern side of **Ponte alle Grazie ❶**. For a coffee before you start, turn left down Via dei Renai for the **Gelateria Vivaldi**, see ❶.

BARDINI MUSEUM

Return towards the bridge and turn left to the small **Museo Stefano Bardini ❷** (Piazza dei Mozzi 1; www.museicivicifiorentini.comune.fi.it; Fri–Mon 11am–5pm). Antiques dealer Stefano Bardini created his *palazzo* over the 13th-century church and monastery of San Gregorio in 1881, incorporating fragments of the ancient buildings. He used the rooms to showcase his vast art collection and bequeathed the palace and contents to the city in 1923. After 15 years of restoration the palace has been returned to its former glory. Among the highlights are Bernardo Daddi's monumental crucifix, a terracotta altarpiece by Andrea della Robbia, a Madonna attributed to Donatello and Pollaiuolo's St Michael. There are also some lovely Persian carpets, Turkish ceramics, musical instruments and suits of armour. Bardini also created the nearby Giardino Bardini, also open to the public.

SAN MINIATO GATEWAY

Turn left down Via di San Niccolò. This threads past imposing palaces and the church of San Niccolò, up to Via San Miniato, where you turn right and pass

San Miniato façade detail

through the **Porta San Miniato ❸**. This is one of the few surviving gateways from the 14th-century city wall. If it is already lunch time, a good place for a bite to eat is the *osteria* **Antica Mescita San Niccolò**, see ❷, just before the arch.

On the other side of the arch turn left up Via dei Bastoni, which follows the wall. A short way up, look for a set of stone steps on the right that leads straight uphill, passing through leafy gardens and interrupted occasionally by the switch-back main road. Keep following these steps and paths as they weave upwards; on a clear day, the views are splendid. If you cannot face the climb, buses nos.12 and 13 run from Rotonda Barbetti up to Piazzale Michelangelo.

PIAZZALE MICHELANGELO

At the top of the series of steps is the

Piazzale Michelangelo's 'David'

Piazzale Michelangelo ❹. The square was laid out in the 19th century and is dotted with reproductions of Michelangelo's sculptures, not to mention scores of tour buses and souvenir stalls. The views are stunning; it is from here that all those classic postcard pictures of the rooftops of Florence are taken.

Carry on up the busy Viale Galileo Galilei to the steps that lead up to the church of San Miniato.

SAN MINIATO AL MONTE

San Miniato al Monte ❺ (www.san miniatoalmonte.it; Mon–Sat 9.30–1pm, 3–7pm/7.30pm in summer, Sun 8.15–7pm/7.30pm in summer), and its convent buildings, is one of the most beautiful churches in Florence. Catch your breath while admiring the views from the terrace in front of the church and studying its delicate façade, which is covered in geometric patterns of green-and-white marble.

The church was built on the site of the tomb of the city's first Christian martyr, St Minias. He was executed in AD 250 during the anti-Christian purges of the Emperor Diocletian and his shrine was replaced by the present church in 1018. It incorporates Corinthian columns and other Roman material.

The interior

The interior has survived more or less in its original state. Frescoes on the aisle walls include a large 14th-century *St Christopher* by an unknown artist. The nave floor has a superb series of marble intarsia panels depicting lions, doves, signs of the zodiac and the date, 1207. To the left of the pulpit, behind an iron grille, is the tomb of the Cardinal of Portugal, who died on a visit to Florence in 1439. Its glazed terracotta ceiling is by Luca della Robbia. The mosaic in the apse (1297), shows Christ, the Virgin and St Minias. Try to time your trip to coincide with the Gregorian chant sung on Sundays and holidays by the monks at 5.30pm and also at 7.15am and 5.45pm on weekdays.

Miniato mausoleum

Behind the church is a small graveyard that dates back to 1839. Family tombs are supplied with electricity to light the 'everlasting lamps', and there are many highly accomplished figures and portraits in stone and bronze of former Florentine citizens.

THE DESCENT

Descend the steps back down to Viale Galileo Galilei and turn left. After about 150m/yds turn right into Via dell'Erta Canina. This winds down the hillside past villas, the **Convento delle Stimmatine** and fields that are filled with flowers in spring. At the bottom of the road turn right then left to the Porta San Miniato. Just before the gateway is the restaurant **Fuori Porta**, see ❸, which makes a pleasant lunch stop.

Thirteenth-century mosaic of Christ inside San Miniato

The Belvedere

To carry on, turn left immediately before Porta San Miniato and walk along Via di Belvedere until it meets Via di San Leonardo. Turn right, then left to bring you out in front of the **Forte di Belvedere ❻**. The sheer and massive walls of this fortress overlook the Boboli Garden. The interior, which is still under restoration and usually closed, is almost empty and only used now for occasional exhibitions.

The fortress was built on the orders of Ferdinando I, beginning in 1590, to Buontalenti's design. Although the structure was said to be part of the city's defences, there was only one means of access – a secret door entered from the Boboli Garden – and so the fort was only for the use of the city's rulers.

ENDING THE WALK

Leave the Belvedere and turn left down Costa di San Giorgio, continuing on when this turns into Costa de' Magnoli and, at Piazza Santa Maria Soprarno, turn left into Via de'Bardi. You are now at the southern end of the Ponte Vecchio. On your right is the **Golden View**, see ❹ – a good place for an *aperitivo*.

Food and drink

❶ GELATERIA VIVALDI

Via dei Renai 15r; tel: 055-234 3185; Sun–Thu 8am–8pm, Fri–Sat until 2am; €

This gelateria serves excellent ice cream, cakes, coffee and hot chocolate. Enjoy your sweet treat in the stylish cosy back room with its elegant sofas and armchairs.

❷ ANTICA MESCITA SAN NICCOLÒ

Via di San Niccolò 60r; tel: 055-234 2836; www.osteriasanniccolo.webnode.it; daily noon–12.30am; €

This *osteria* does simple, cheap but delicious Italian food served up in a cheery, crowded atmosphere. Part of the eatery is set in a former chapel.

❸ FUORI PORTA

Via dei Monte Alle Croci 10r; tel: 055-234 2483; www.fuoriporta.it; Mon–Fri noon–3.30pm, 7–11.30pm, Sat–Sun noon–11.30pm; €€

A little *enoteca* 'outside the gate' whose communal seating adds to the jovial atmosphere. Its much-praised classic Tuscan dishes are rustic and plentiful.

❹ GOLDEN VIEW

Via de'Bardi 58r; tel: 055-214 502; www.goldenviewopenbar.com; daily noon–midnight; €€€

This attractive restaurant/pizzeria/ *enoteca* overlooking the Arno is popular with tourists, especially at *aperitivo* time or when the live jazz strikes up. Cuisine is Tuscan with French and Mediterranean additions. Reservations are advised.

FIESOLE

This small village close to Florence, on the hills overlooking the city, has long attracted those in the city looking for a little peace away from the urban bustle and, during the summer, cooler air.

DISTANCE: 4km (2.5 miles)
TIME: A full day
START: Piazza Mino
END: Badia Fiesolana
POINTS TO NOTE: Buses from Florence to Fiesole run about three to four times an hour and the journey takes about 30 mins. The final stop is Fiesole Vinandro Osteria, close to Piazza Mino. Although you can get the bus back down again from Piazza Mino, it is far more pleasant to follow the route to the end, walking part of the way back down.

Fiesole is a favourite retreat for Florentines, who find the air in this hilltop village fresher than in the valley bottom, where their own city sits. Once, however, relations between the two places were not so comfortable. Fiesole predates Florence by some eight centuries; it was an Etruscan city well before the Romans colonised the area and founded the town from which Florence grew. Thereafter, Fiesole declined, but it remained an important trade competitor until 1125, when Florentine troops stormed it and destroyed all the buildings except for the cathedral.

From the 15th century onwards, numerous fine villas were built on the slopes leading up to Fiesole. Later, they were rented by a growing Anglo-Florentine community, which, in the 19th century, included the poets Robert and Elizabeth Barrett Browning. The Brownings praised its beauty in their poetry, and here, unlike in Florence itself, there was space for the English to indulge their passion for gardening. Standing at nearly 295m (1,000ft) above sea level, Fiesole was considered more salubrious than the furnace of Florence (in fact the difference is marginal).

TOWARDS PIAZZA MINO

You will see these villas from the bus as you approach Fiesole. To get there from central Florence, take bus no. 7 from Stazione Nationale, buying your ticket

The Teatro Romano enjoys glorious views

from one of the ticket machines or cafés by the bus stop. The short journey from the city ends at the **Piazza Mino ❶**, Fiesole's broad, main square, which occupies the site of the Roman forum.

ROMAN AMPHITHEATRE

From Piazza Mino head north across the square, to the right of the cathedral, to the entrance to the **Teatro Romano** and **Area Archeologica ❷** (tel: 055-596 1293; www.museidifiesole.it; daily Apr–Sept 9am–7pm, Mar and Oct 10am–6pm, Nov–Feb Wed–Mon 10am–3pm; combination ticket includes Fiesole's other museums). The impeccably preserved amphitheatre, with a seating capacity of around 3,000, is the site of a popular arts festival held in June and July (see page 120). The larger blocks of stone represent original Roman seats, the smaller ones modern replacements. The site enjoys stunning views over the low, cypress-topped hills of the Mugello region to the north. Surrounding the theatre are the jumbled remains of Etruscan and Roman temples and baths. The small but nonetheless excellent **Museo Archeologico**, in the same complex, displays tiny Etruscan figures (dancers, warriors, orators), sensual, headless statues of Dionysos and Venus and many other notable sculptures. The building is an imaginative reconstruction of the 1st-century BC Roman temple, whose excavated remains are in the northwestern area of the theatre complex; parts of the original Roman frieze are incorporated into the pediment.

BANDINI MUSEUM

Almost directly opposite the entrance to the Teatro Romano, in Via Dupré, the **Museo Bandini ❸** (www.museidifiesole.it; Fri–Sun Apr–Sept 9am–7pm, Mar and Oct 10am–6pm, Nov–Feb 10am–3pm; same ticket as the Area Archeologica) has an outstanding collection of paintings by the so-called Italian Primitives. This name was given to artists such as Taddeo and Agnolo Gaddi and Nardo di Cione, who continued to work in the Gothic idiom well into the Renaissance era. Most of the paintings are religious, but there is an extremely rare and unusual late 15th-century allegorical work by Jacopo del Sellaio showing the *Triumph of Love, Time, Chastity and Piety*.

SAN ROMOLO CATHEDRAL

Head back to Piazza Mino, and, on your right, is the **Cattedrale di San Romolo ❹** (daily 7.30am–noon and 3–6pm, Nov–Mar 7.30am–noon and 2–5pm). The apse of this severe, sandstone basilica contains 16th-century frescoes by local artist Nicodemo Ferrucci; they depict the life of St Romolo, whose sarcophagus is in the crypt below. The highlight of the church, however, is the tomb that Mino da Fiesole designed for the humanist Bishop Leonardo Salutati.

The arches of the Teatro Romano

SAN IACOPO CHAPEL

Look for Via San Francesco, which climbs steeply opposite the cathedral façade. A short way up is the **Cappella di San Iacopo ❺** (Sat and Sun by appointment only, tel: 55-591 118), containing ecclesiastical treasures and early crucifixes. Further up, a terrace gives sweeping views over Florence.

SANT'ALESSANDRO

At the top of the lane is **Sant'Alessandro ❻**, whose plain, squat façade hides a 6th-century basilica with re-used Roman columns of green-veined *cipollino* (onion-ring) marble. It is the church of the friary of **San Francesco ❼** (daily Apr–Sept 9am–noon and 3–7pm, Oct–Mar until 6pm) and was constructed on the site of an exposed section of the 3rd-century BC Etruscan city wall.

It has been a monastery since the 15th century, and a monk will let you in to go upstairs and inspect the barren cells in which these holy men spent most of their lives. The church itself is packed with works of art, and, off the cloister, there is a curious museum full of dusty relics collected in China and Egypt by Franciscan missionaries.

Summer flowers in Fiesole

Close by is **La Reggia degli Etruschi**, see ❶, which boasts more great views.

BACK TO FLORENCE

You can now catch the bus back from Piazza Mino or walk part of the way, following the narrow Via Vecchia Fiesolana out of the square. En route you will pass the **Villa Medici** ❽ (www.villa medicifiesole.it; Mon−Fri 9am−1pm; gardens only by appointment at annamarchimazzini@gmail.com), built by Michelozzo in 1458, and a favourite retreat of Lorenzo de'Medici. Its gardens, and the view from its terraces, are superb. In 2013 the Villa Medici became a Unesco World Heritage Site, alongside 11 other Tuscan Medici villas and two gardens. On the descent, you can enjoy glimpses of other villas behind their high walls and note various examples of stonework and the typical Tuscan cypress trees.

The next stop on the route, after just 1km (0.5 mile), is the convent of **San Domenico** ❾ (daily summer 7.30am−12.30pm and 4.30−6.30pm, winter 8.30am−noon and 4−6pm), home to Fra Angelico's *Madonna with Angels* (1430) in the church and his *Crucifixion* (also from 1430) in the Chapter House. Fra Angelico began his monastic life here before transferring to San Marco (see page 58).

From here, take the left fork down to the **Badia Fiesolana** ❿ (Mon−Fri 9am−5.30pm, Sat 9am−noon), the church that served as Fiesole's cathedral until 1058. The original Romanesque façade, which is framed by the rough, unfinished stonework of the enlarged 15th-century church, is a delicate work of inlaid marble.

There is another magnificent view over Florence from the terrace in front of the church.

Return to the Convent of San Domenico for the bus stop outside the church where the No. 7 bus will pick you up on the way back to Florence. If you fancy something to eat beforehand, then on Piazza San Domenico is the **Pizzeria San Domenico**, see ❷.

Food and drink

❶ LA REGGIA DEGLI ETRUSCHI
Via San Francesco 18; tel: 055-59385; www.lareggiadeglietruschi.com; daily 12.30−2pm, 7−10pm; €€
The patio here offers a wonderful view over Florence spread out below. The food might not be quite as breathtaking as the view, but it's good, solid Italian fare nonetheless.

❷ PIZZERIA SAN DOMENICO
Piazza San Domenico 11; tel: 055-59182; www.pizzeriasandomenico.it; daily noon−3pm, 7pm−midnight; €€
This is a simple restaurant with a huge selection of pizzas and pastas, and friendly service. Try one of the big salads followed by a *coppa della casa* (the house dessert).

Villa Medicea della Petraia

MEDICI VILLAS

Not content with their sumptuous palaces and art works in Florence itself, the Medici built themselves beautiful residences in the countryside around the city. This route visits two of the finest.

DISTANCE: 2.5km (1.5 miles)
TIME: A full day
START: Villa Corsini
END: Villa Medicea Poggio ai Caiano
POINTS TO NOTE: Both villas are easily seen in one day (the Villa della Petraia in the morning and the Poggio ai Caiano in the afternoon), though each half of the route could also be done separately. The gardens of the Villa della Petraia are lovely for a picnic; instead of eating back in town, you might want to pick up some edibles at the Mercato Centrale (see page 54) before you leave.

This tour is great for anyone with an interest in history and architecture, as well as garden-lovers, but do not expect colourful herbaceous borders: the two gardens to be visited were laid out in the formal Italian style in the 16th century and are of great historical interest. They can be enjoyed in all seasons. The garden of the Villa Medicea della Petraia is backed by extensive woodland, which is perfect for picnicking.

The style of these Renaissance Tuscan houses is representative of the peaceful period and ideal of gracious living that prevailed over Florence at the time. The villas are generally centred around an inner courtyard and feature porticoes and a loggia, but the centrepieces – often open even if the house is closed – are arguably the gardens. These reflect architectural rigour in their design and feature sculptures and fountains similar to those seen in the Boboli Garden (see page 74).

Many of the villas are now privately owned or have been transformed into American university campuses, thereby restricting what can be viewed and rendering the opening hours erratic. Most villas are accessible by a short bus ride out of Florence, although some companies organise trips by coach to combine visits.

In 2013, 12 Tuscan Medici villas and two gardens became Unesco World Heritage Sites, including the Villa Medicea

'The Clash' painting in Villa Corsini

della Petraia and the Villa Medicea Poggio ai Caiano.

Catching the bus

To reach them, take bus no. 2 or 28 from Piazza Dalmazia (www.ataf.net). Buses leave around every 15 minutes, and tickets can be bought from the machine by the bus stop.

The journey takes about 15 minutes, and, if possible, ask the driver to let you know where to get off for the Villa Medicea della Petraia. Alternatively, keep an eye on where you are going. The bus heads north to the suburb of Rifredi, then follows the railway track along the long Via Reginaldo Giuliani and the Via Sestese. Get off at stop 'Sestese 03'. Walk back a little way and turn left up Via Collodi; at the top turn right into Via Reginaldo Giuliani and then left up the narrow Via della Petraia.

VILLA CORSINI

About 500m (0.25 mile) up the lane you will pass the **Villa Corsini** ❶ (www.polomusealetoscana.beniculturali.it; days and hours vary) with its cream-coloured Baroque façade and a plaque recording that Robert Dudley died here on 6 September 1649.

Dudley, the illegitimate son of the Earl of Leicester (Queen Elizabeth I's favourite) was the leading marine engineer of his age and was employed by Cosimo I to build the harbour at Livorno (Tuscany's principal port).

The formal garden of the Villa Corsini (only open to the public for special events) was laid out for Duke Cosimo I in 1541 and was once regarded as the supreme example of Renaissance gardening. The real point of your visit, however, lies a little further on.

Superb gardens and views at the Villa Medicea della Petraia

VILLA MEDICEA DELLA PETRAIA

The **Villa Medicea della Petraia** ❷ (www.polomusealetoscana.beniculturali.it; daily, gardens: 8.30am–sunset; villa: by guided tour only every hour from 8.30am, closed 2nd and 3rd Mon of the month) is another 1km (0.5 mile) up from here.

Enter the gate and take the first entrance in the wall on the right. You'll pass into the garden (laid out with flower beds enclosed by low box hedges) that fronts the villa. Like many Italian gardens in the 18th century, these were designed in the style of English parkland. Take the central path up some steps and past a large fish pond to the terrace in front of the villa. From here the scroll work and geometric patterning of the box parterre can best be appreciated. There are also good views from here; left to the dome of Florence cathedral, straight ahead to the new industrial suburb of Firenze Nuova and right to the city's Peretola airport.

The interior

Individual visitors can wander around the garden at will, but tours of the villa itself are only given to groups of 10, so you may have to wait and team up with other visitors (then press the bell to be let in).

The main attraction inside is the central hallway, which is covered in frescoes detailing the history of the Medici. The villa was built as a fortress (whose tower still stands), then turned into a country mansion in the 1570s by Grand Duke Ferdinand I. It was altered again in the 19th century under the Savoys.

Also during the 19th century, Villa Medicea della Petraia was the favourite residence of the King of Italy, Victor Emmanuel II and it was he who had the tree house constructed in the huge (and now dead) ilex oak to the left of the villa's façade.

The park

To the right of the villa, a gate in the wall leads to a large park full of ilex and cypress trees – offering cool respite even in the heat of summer – and threaded with little streams. This juxtaposition of the highly formal garden with wild and mysterious woodland was a favourite, and very effective, device of Italian gardeners from the Renaissance onwards.

To return to Florence, retrace your steps to Via Sestese, cross the (usually busy) road and look for the bus stop down on the right (again buses nos. 2 and 28 will take you back to Piazza Dalmazia).

TO POGGIO AI CAIANO

Once back in Florence, you can either grab something to eat on Piazza Santa Maria Novella or at the Mercato Centrale or, if you have already had a picnic at Villa della Petraia, head straight off for the second of the two villas.

To reach Poggio ai Caiano, which is actually just over the boundary in the

Villa Medicea Poggio ai Caiano

province of neighbouring Prato, 11 miles (18km) northwest of Florence, take one of the CAP buses from Santa Maria Novella (www.capautolinee.it). They depart every 25 minutes or so, and the journey takes about half an hour.

Villa Medicea Poggio ai Caiano

Alight at the stop on top of the small rise just outside the villa; either ask the driver to tell you when to get off, or keep a look out for the large walls enclosing the villa's gardens. This is the entrance to the **Villa Medicea Poggio ai Caiano** ❸ (www.polomuseale toscana.beniculturali.it; daily, gardens: 8.15am–sunset; villa: by guided tour only, hourly from 8.30am, closed 2nd and 3rd Mon of the month).

Often considered to be the 'most perfect' of the Medici's out-of-town residences, the villa has beautiful proportions. Its façade, by Sangallo, was modelled on a Greek temple on the instructions of Lorenzo the Magnificent. Above the main entrance, along the portico, is a glazed terracotta frieze by Andrea della Robbia.

The interior has been well restored. The highlights of the tour are the ground-floor private theatre, where the Medici were entertained by the leading actors of the day; and the large central hall upstairs with its superb frescoes.

The gardens are in two parts. To the front and side are the formal Italianate gardens with their large trees, carefully manicured flower beds and the lovely orangerie. Behind the villa is an attractive area of landscaped parkland, which is bounded by a small stream.

BACK TO FLORENCE

Once you have finished your tour of the villa and its gardens, then you have a choice: either take the bus straight back into town and find something to eat, or head just down the hill (back towards Florence).

On the left is Piazza XX Settembre, where you can have an early dinner at **Il Falcone**, see ❶. This is ideal for a late lunch or early dinner after seeing the villa, but before sitting down to an evening meal first check the times of buses back to Florence.

Food and drink

❶ IL FALCONE

Piazza XX Settembre 35, Poggio a Caiano; tel: 055-877 065; www.ristoranteilfalcone. com; Thu–Tue noon–2pm and 7.30–9.30pm; €€

This welcoming little restaurant dates back to the mid-19th century and has been in the same family for seven generations. It specialises in straightforward rustic local dishes, such as *pappardelle* with goose, or wild boar, *ribollita* and excellent *trippa alla fiorentina*. One fish dish is served every Friday. The wine list offers an excellent selection of Chiantis and Super Tuscans.

San Gimignano 'skyscrapers'

SAN GIMIGNANO

This hilltop village, about halfway between Florence and Pisa, is one of Tuscany's most famous sights. Only 13 of the town's original 76 towers remain, but San Gimignano is still Italy's best-preserved medieval village.

DISTANCE: 3km (2 miles)
TIME: A full day
START: Porta San Giovanni
END: The Rocca
POINTS TO NOTE: Arrive in San Gimignano as early as possible, before the tour buses arrive. Even better, stay overnight to see the village at its best during the evening and early morning.

San Gimignano is a very popular excursion from Florence and easily reached by public transport. Take the Busitalia San Gimignano bus (the ticket office is at Via Santa Caterina da Siena 17r) from Santa Maria Novella station (www.fsbusitalia.it); it departs every hour and connects at Poggibonsi for another bus ride (www.trainspa.it) up to San Gimignano itself. The whole journey takes about 1.5 hours, depending on the connection.

From Poggibonsi the approach is memorable, as the town's towers – the so-called *belle torri*, originally designed as keeps during the Guelf–Ghibelline feuds in the 12th and 13th centuries –

come into view behind the olive trees, cypress trees and vines.

Arriving at **Porta San Giovanni ❶**, walk up Via San Giovanni to **Piazza della Cisterna ❷**. This lovely triangular square is named after its 13th-century well and lined with medieval *palazzi*. Also here is the **Gelateria Dondoli**, see ❶.

PIAZZA DEL DUOMO

Just beyond is the asymmetrical Piazza del Duomo, site of the **Palazzo Comunale ❸** (www.museicivicifiorentini.comune.fi.it; daily Apr–Sept 10am–7.30pm, Oct–Mar

---

Food and drink

❶ GELATERIA DONDOLI

Piazza della Cisterna 4; tel: 0577-942 244; www.gelateriadondoli.com; daily 9am–11pm; €

This award-winning *gelateria* is well worth a visit: try the *dolceamaro* made with herbs, chocolate and coffee, or the *sorbetto al mosto* (made with wine must).

Passeggiata in the streets of San Gimignano

11am–5.30pm), with its 54-m (177ft) Torre Grossa, completed in around 1300. In the same square is the **Museo Civico** ❹ (same times and ticket as the Palazzo Comunale) with an excellent collection of works by Florentine and Sienese masters, including pieces by Gozzoli, Lippi, Taddeo di Bartolo and Giotto.

On the far left-hand corner of the square is the Romanesque **Collegiata** (or Duomo) ❺ (www.duomosangimignano. it; Apr–Oct Mon–Fri 10am–7.30pm, Sat 10am–5.30pm, Sun 12.30–7.30pm, Nov–Mar Mon–Sat 10am–5pm, Sun 12.30–5pm, closed second half of Jan and Nov). Although this is the 'Duomo' after which the square is named, it no longer has the status of a cathedral because there is no resident bishop.

The plain façade belies the gloriously lavish interior; vaulted ceilings painted with gold stars and walls covered in fine frescoes. Look out for Bartolo di Fredi's Old Testament scenes along the north aisle, and Barna di Siena's New Testament scenes on the south wall.

THE ROCCA

Continue on past the northern side of the Collegiata, turn left and then right, following a short road up to the **Rocca** ❻. This ruined 14th-century fortress offers a splendid view over the village and countryside.

The bus back to Florence leaves from Porta San Giovanni so you will need to retrace your steps. From Mon–Sat the last bus is at 8.35pm and on Sundays at 7.40pm.

Il Campo during the twice-annual Palio

SIENA

This is a full day exploring the attractive medieval city of Siena, the arch-rival of Florence, with whom it fought many battles. Siena's art and architecture are superb – the glorious main square alone makes it worth a visit.

> **DISTANCE:** 1.5km (1 mile)
> **TIME:** A full day
> **START:** Il Campo
> **END:** Pinacoteca Nazionale
> **POINTS TO NOTE:** Siena is a full day trip from Florence, but a relatively easy one, with the trains running late enough to allow for dinner in Siena.

According to legend, the city of Siena was founded by Senius, son of Remus; hence the she-wolf symbols seen around the city. There is a long history – starting in the 12th century – of rivalry between the (usually triumphant) Florentine Guelfs and the Sienese Ghibellines. Everywhere there are reminders of this longstanding enmity, both in Siena and in the strategically placed fortified towns scattered throughout its province.

The city is divided into three districts or *terzi* (thirds) – the Terzo di Città, Terzo di San Martino and Terzo di Camollia. But this is purely administrative: Siena's true identity is inextricably linked to the *contrade*, the 17 medieval districts from which its social fabric is woven.

Arrival

Trains leave from Santa Maria Novella every 30 mins (www.trenitalia.com), with the journey lasting 90–110 minutes and last train returning at 9.40pm. The bus can be faster: Busitalia coaches (www.fsbusitalia.it) leave every 30 minutes in high season. The trip takes 75 minutes. From the train station, take a local bus (nos 3 or 10; www.sienamobilita.it) for the 10-minute journey to Via Tozzi (Busitalia buses stop here), then walk down Via Montanini and Via Bianchi di Sopra to reach **Il Campo ❶**, Siena's main square.

IL CAMPO

This beautiful space – Il Campo, or Piazza del Campo – spreads out from the Gothic town hall like a fan, with the Fonte Gaia fountain at its tip. Cobblestones divide the piazza into nine segments, meant to represent the Governo dei Nove (Council of the Nine), an oligarchy of merchants who ruled the medieval city until the end of its

The race in full swing

golden age in 1355. It was during their rule that the finest works of Sienese art and architecture were commissioned or completed, including the Campo and the **Palazzo Pubblico ❷**.

PALAZZO PUBBLICO

Considered to be one of the most beautiful Gothic buildings in Tuscany, this *palazzo* contains the **Museo Civico** (daily Nov–mid-Mar 10am–6pm, mid-Mar–Oct until 7pm), which is more a fabulously decorated palace than a classic museum. The main council chamber is adorned with Simone Mar-

tini's *Maestà* – depicting the Madonna on a filigree throne – and his celebrated fresco of a *condottiere* (mercenary).

For a glorious view of the piazza and the rooftops, climb the **Torre del Mangia** but be prepared to queue. At 102m (335ft) the belltower is the second highest in Italy. The **Cappella in Piazza** (Chapel in the Square) at the bottom of the tower was erected in 1378 in thanksgiving for the end of the plague. You will find the statue of the Mangia, the gluttonous bell-ringer that the tower is named after, in the Cortile del Podestà, the courtyard that lies next to the chapel. Before carrying on, you might like to eat on the square at **Al Man-**

The 'zebra-striped' Duomo

gia, see ❶, or just behind it at **Osteria Il Carroccio**, see ❷.

THE DUOMO

From the Campo, head south past the Palazzo Chigi-Saracini and then turn right and then left into Via di Città.

Carry on to the next turning on the right and walk straight down to Siena's wonderful cathedral, the **Duomo** ❸ (www.operaduomo.siena.

The Palio

Siena's famous horse race, the Palio, takes place twice annually and lasts just 90 seconds but it is the highlight of the year for many of the city's inhabitants. The Palio (www.ilpalio.org) has been held since the 13th century, when the August Palio made its debut. At that time, the contest took the form of a bareback race the length of the city. The race run around the Piazza del Campo was introduced in the 17th century and today takes place on 2 July and 16 August. The costume parade, which is staged in the run-up to the main race, retraces Siena's centuries of struggle against Florence, from the glorious victory against its arch-rival in 1260 to the ghastly defeat in 1560. The race then begins and hurtles around the Campo three times. If a riderless horse wins, the animal is almost deified: it is given the place of honour in the victory banquet and has its hooves painted gold.

it; Mar–Oct 10.30am–7pm, Nov–Feb 10.30am–5.30pm; combined ticket with the Museo dell'Opera del Duomo and Battistero San Giovanni).

Part riotous Gothic and part austere Romanesque, the Duomo is perched on one of Siena's three hills. The interior is an equally dazzling mix of styles with its soaring black-and-white pillars and inlaid marble floors. The exquisite pulpit was carved by Niccolò Pisano and the Libreria Piccolomini holds the illuminated manuscripts of Pope Pius II. The frescoes by Pinturicchio (1509) depict scenes from the life of the influential Renaissance pope, a member of the noble Sienese Piccolomini family and founder of Renaissance Pienza.

Cathedral Museum

In the eastern section of the Duomo, unfinished because of the Black Death, is the **Museo dell'Opera del Duomo** ❹ (www.operaduomo.siena.it; same hours as Duomo). The museum is famed for its marble statues carved by Giovanni Pisano for the façade, and for Duccio's altarpiece of *The Virgin and Child Enthroned in Majesty*, or *Maestà* (1308–11).

Baptistry

Continuing on around the northern edge of the Duomo to Piazza San Giovanni brings you to the **Battistero San Giovanni** ❺ (same hours as Duomo). Built in 1316–25, the Baptistry has a tall Gothic façade. The superb interior is adorned with frescoes by, among others, Lorenzo di Pietro (Vecchietta). The font (1431) has

Piazza Salinbeni   *Rooftop view of Siena*

gilded bronze bas-reliefs by Jacopo della Quercia, Donatello and Ghiberti.

SANTA MARIA DELLA SCALA

On the far side of the Duomo the **Santa Maria della Scala** ❻ (www.santa mariadellascala.com; mid-Mar–mid-Oct, Fri–Wed 10am–7pm, Thu until 10pm, mid-Oct–mid-Mar, Mon, Wed, Fri 10am–5pm, Thu until 8pm, Sat–Sun until 7pm, Dec 23rd–Jan 6th, Fri–Wed 10am–7pm, Thu until 8pm, last entry 30 mins before closing) is the former pilgrims' hospital, in its heyday one of the most important hospitals in the world. Much of the vast complex has been restored and turned into a cultural centre. The main ward, the Sala Pellegrinaio, boasts stunning frescoes by Domenico di Bartolo narrating the history of the hospital. The old hayloft or *fienile* now houses Jacopo della Quercia's original sculpted panels from the *Fonte Gaia* (Fountain of Joy) in Siena's Campo. Other highlights are the Oratorio di Santa Caterina della Notte, the Church of Santissima Annunziata and the city's architectural museum.

PINACOTECA NAZIONALE

Take Via del Capitano south from the piazza. About 200m/yds further on is the **Pinacoteca Nazionale** ❼ (National Gallery; www.pinacotecanazionale.siena. it; Tue–Sat 8.15am–7.15pm, Sun–Mon 9am–1pm). This collection, housed in the suitably Gothic Palazzo Buonsignori,

holds great works of art from the Siena School, famed for its *fondi d'oro*: paintings with lavish, gilded backgrounds.

From here it is easy to head back to Il Campo along Via Casato di Sopra. A good place to eat in the vicinity is the **Trattoria Papei**, see ❸.

Food and drink

❶ AL MANGIA
Il Campo 42; tel: 0577-281 121; www. almangia.it; daily noon–10.30pm; €€€€
In a wonderful position on the Campo, Al Mangia serves classic Tuscan cuisine popular with locals. Outside tables in summer. You pay a premium for the location, but it is worth it.

❷ OSTERIA IL CARROCCIO
Via Casato di Sotto 32; tel: 0577-41165; Thu–Tue 12.15–2.45pm and 7.15–9.45pm; €
A well-run, quaint and tiny *trattoria* serving simple local dishes. Friendly and cosy. Outdoor dining available.

❸ TRATTORIA PAPEI
Piazza del Mercato 6; tel: 0577-280 894; www.anticatrattoriapapei.com; daily noon–10.30pm; €€
This is an ideal place for Sienese home cooking, such as *pappardelle al sugo di cinghiale* (pasta in wild boar sauce) or *pici alla cardinale* (pasta in a hot tomato sauce with *pancetta*), as well as good grilled meat plates.

The Duomo

PISA

15

This easy excursion from Florence takes in Pisa's essential sights. The crowds of tourists are inevitable, but do not detract too much from the enjoyment of the world-famous Leaning Tower, cathedral, Baptistry and Camposanto.

DISTANCE: 5km (3 miles)
TIME: A full day
START: Piazza dei Cavalieri
END: Santa Maria della Spina
POINTS TO NOTE: The best way to get to Pisa is by train. Trains run regularly from Santa Maria Novella station (see www.trenitalia.com for times) and fares are cheap. Be prepared for long queues at the Leaning Tower. You can reserve tickets 1–20 days in advance at www.opapisa.it for no extra cost. Children under 8 are not allowed up the tower and those aged 8–18 must be accompanied by an adult.

Many visitors to Florence arrive and depart from Pisa's Galileo Galilei airport, but do not find time to visit Pisa itself. This is a pity, since it is very easy to reach from Florence, and its sights are memorable. This is the birthplace of Galileo, and home of the fabled Leaning Tower. Pisa was a flourishing commercial centre and port during the Middle Ages, until the silting-up of

the Arno estuary left it stranded 11km (7 miles) inland from the coast.

Trains depart from Santa Maria Novella station in Florence roughly every half hour and the journey takes just over an hour. The train follows the Arno valley downstream, calling first at the industrial town of Empoli, before arriving at Pisa Centrale station.

To the Arno

Leave the station, head straight up Viale Gramsci, crossing the busy Piazza Vittorio Emanuele and continuing up Corso Italia. This brings you to the banks of the River Arno, which is much wider here than in Florence. Cross the Ponte di Mezzo to Piazza Garibaldi and walk up the arcaded Borgo Stretto, Pisa's animated main shopping street. Take the first left, Via Ulisse Dini, to reach the **Piazza dei Cavalieri ❶** (Square of the Knights).

PIAZZA DEI CAVALIERI

This square is dominated by the Palazzo della Carovana, built by Vasari in 1562

The famous tower, with cherub statue

Rising tiers of colonnades decorate the Duomo

and covered in black-and-white *sgraffito* decoration, featuring signs of the Zodiac and mythical figures. The *palazzo* (now a secondary school) stands on the site of Pisa's original *municipio* (town hall), which was demolished in 1509 to symbolise the subjugation of Pisa after the city had been defeated by the powerful Florentines.

Santo Stefano

A large statue of Duke Cosimo I stands in front of the palace. To the right, the church of **Santo Stefano dei Cavalieri** ❷ (Apr–Nov daily 9am–6pm, Oct–Mar Mon–Sat 11am–4.30pm, Sun 11.30am–5.30pm) holds war trophies captured by the crusading *cavalieri* (knights) of St Stephen in battles against the Turks.

Just to the left is the **Palazzo dell' Orologio** (Palace of the Clock), which incorporates the grim **Torre Gualandi**, known as the Tower of Hunger. This is where Count Ugolino, along with all his sons and grandsons, was walled up and starved to death in 1288 for

allegedly betraying Pisa to the Genoese. The tragic story is told both in Dante's *Inferno* (Canto XXXIII) and in Percy Bysshe Shelley's 1820 poem, *The Tower of Famine*.

A few streets from the square is a good place for something to eat: the **Trattoria Sant'Omobono**, see ①.

FIELD OF MIRACLES

Pass under the arch beneath the clock tower and take the right-hand street, Via Martiri. This bends left to join Via Cardinale Capponi, which leads to the **Campo dei Miracoli** ❸ (Field of Miracles), where the famous ensemble of Pisa's Torre Pendente (Leaning Tower), the cathedral and the Baptistry is revealed. No matter how many photographs you may have seen, nothing prepares you for the impact of these extraordinary buildings when seen at first hand.

Pisa was a thriving port (until the mouth of the Arno silted up in the 16th century), and the city had extensive trade contacts with Spain and North Africa during the 12th and 13th centuries. This explains the Moorish influence on the architecture of these buildings, which is evident in the marble arabesque patterns that cover the walls of the cathedral and the bristling, minaret-like pinnacles of the Baptistry. All of the buildings tilt (because of badly built foundations), not just the Leaning Tower, so you may

Pisan Regatta

In mid-June Pisa holds its Regatta di San Ranieri, when boat races and processions of decorated boats are held on the River Arno. The evening before the regatta, tens of thousands of candles and torches are placed on the buildings along the river – a stunning sight.

Quirky Pisan postbox

experience sensations of vertigo if you look at them for too long.

The ticket office for these buildings is to the right, beside the Leaning Tower. Various combinations are on offer, depending on which monuments you want to visit.

LEANING TOWER

The **Torre Pendente** ❹ (www.opapisa.it; daily Jan and Dec 10am–5pm, Feb and Nov 9.45am–5.15pm, Mar 9am–6pm, Apr–Sept 9am–8pm, Oct 9am–7pm; 30-minute guided tours; tickets from ticket office behind tower or Museo delle Sinopie on south side of the Campo dei Miracoli), begun in 1173, started to tilt during the early stages of construction, when it was only 10.5m (35ft) high. Some people like to joke that the Pisans deliberately built it this way, so as to ensure a healthy income from tourism in years to come. Completed in 1350, the tower has continued to slide, and now, at 54.5m (180ft) high, it leans 4.5m (15ft) from the perpendicular. An ambitious 10-year underpinning programme has stabilised the tower and visitors are once again allowed to climb it. Fifty people are permitted to climb the 297 steps every 15 minutes.

THE DUOMO

The **Duomo** ❺ (Cathedral; www.opapisa.it; daily Nov–Feb 10am–6pm, Mar until 7pm, Apr–Oct 10am–8pm) alongside the tower is as interesting for its exterior as its interior. It was begun in 1063, and the façade is covered in rising tiers of colonnades that are typical of the distinctive Pisan Romanesque style. The bronze doors below date from 1602 and illustrate various biblical scenes. Buscheto, the original architect of the Duomo, combined the ground plan of an early Christian basilica with a transept, making this the first sacred building built in the shape of a cross in Italy. He was also familiar with Islamic architecture, and used arches inside and intarsia decoration on the exterior.

The cathedral is entered through the south transept, which also has important Romanesque bronze doors, designed by Bonnano da Pisa in 1180; these illustrate scenes from the Life of Christ.

The interior

Fire devastated the interior in 1595 but spared Cimabue's mosaic of *Christ in Majesty* (1302) in the vault of the apse and the outstanding pulpit, carved with New Testament scenes. This is the work of the father-and-son team, Niccolò and Giovanni Pisano. Although it dates from the 13th century, when Gothic was the predominant style, their style anticipates the best Renaissance sculpture of the following century.

BAPTISTRY

You will see more proto-Renaissance sculpture in the **Battistero** ❻ (daily Nov–Feb 9am–6pm, Mar until 7pm, Apr–Oct 8am–8pm). The Baptistry was designed and completed by the Pisani in 1284 and contains Niccolò Pisano's first important work, the fine pulpit with panels carved with animated scenes from the Life of Christ.

HOLY FIELD

Giorgio Vasari, the great 16th-century art historian, informs us that the Pisani were influenced by the carvings on the Roman sarcophagi that are to be found in the **Camposanto** ❼ (Holy Field; daily Nov–Feb 9am–6pm, Mar until 7pm, Apr–Jun, Sept–Oct 8am–8pm, Jul–Aug 8am–10pm), the cemetery that lies to the north of the cathedral and is enclosed by marble walls. This was begun in 1278, and shiploads of soil were brought back from the Holy Land in Pisan ships, along with the sarcophagi, to add sanctity to the burial ground.

The cloister walls around the cemetery were once gloriously frescoed, but they were damaged when a stray Allied bomb hit the cemetery in 1944. Even so, fragments remain of a lively Last Judgement by an unknown 14th-century artist.

Before carrying on to the nearby museums you may want some lunch.

Two options just a short walk away are the **Osteria i Santi**, see ❷, and the **Antica Trattoria da Bruno**, see ❸.

PISAN MUSEUMS

On the south side of the Campo dei Miracoli is the **Museo delle Sinopie** ❽ (daily Nov–Feb 9am–6pm, Mar until 7pm, Apr–Oct 8am–8pm), which is where the remaining frescoes from the Camposanto are on display. Many consist of nothing more than the *sinopie*, the preliminary designs sketched into the plaster undercoat to guide the artist during the final stage, when the finished fresco is painted onto the moist final coat of plaster.

Also of interest is the **Museo dell'Opera del Duomo** ❾ (www.operaduomo.firenze.it; closed for restoration) on the corner of the Piazza del Duomo nearest to the Leaning Tower. This museum contains numerous works of art, including Giovanni Pisano's exquisite ivory *Virgin and Child*. The museum's courtyard also offers an unusual view of the Leaning Tower.

ROMANESQUE AND GOTHIC CHURCHES

You can retrace your steps back to the station from here if you want to go straight back to Florence, or extend the route via two churches with exceptional exterior decoration. From

Santa Maria della Spina, along the Arno

Piazza del Duomo, take Via Roma southwards, passing the **Orto Botanico** (Botanical Garden) on your left until you reach the Arno embankment.

At this point, you could cross over the Ponte Solferino and turn right along Lungarno Sidney Sonnino to reach the church of **San Paolo a Ripa d'Arno**, which has a fine Pisan Romanesque façade. For the main walk, however, turn left into Lungarno Gambacorti after the bridge, towards the recently restored **Santa Maria della Spina** ❿ (Nov–Feb Tue–Sun 10am–2pm, Mar–Oct Tue–Fri 10am–1.30pm, 2.30–6pm, Sat–Sun 10am–1.30pm, 2.30–7pm).

This 14th-century Gothic church was built to house a single thorn from Christ's Crown of Thorns, brought to the church in 1333. This theme is picked up by the bristling exterior, covered with prickly pinnacles and niches containing statues of Christ, the Virgin and the Apostles, and gives the church its name. However, the thorn no longer resides here, it is on show in the Chiesa di Santa Chiara on Via Roma.

A right turn after the church will take you down Via Sant'Antonio and back to Pisa Centrale station, from where you can take the train back to Florence.

Food and drink

❶ TRATTORIA SANT'OMOBONO

Piazza Sant'Omobono 6; tel: 050-540 847; Mon–Sat 12.30–2.30pm, 7.30–10pm; €€

This decent little restaurant, not far from Piazza dei Cavalieri, serves good local food. Among the dishes are roast pork, salt cod and pasta with local sausage. The interior has a nicely antique feel, and the service is friendly.

❷ OSTERIA I SANTI

Via Santa Maria 71; tel: 050-28081; www.osteria-isanti.com; Tue–Sun noon–3pm, 7–11pm; €

Away from the tourist traps around the Campo dei Miracoli, this family-run restaurant is about a 10-minute walk away to the south. The food comprises simple, straightforward Tuscan dishes that are perfectly adequate and very reasonably priced.

❸ ANTICA TRATTORIA DA BRUNO

Via Luigi Bianchi 12; tel: 050-560 818; Thu–Mon noon–3pm, 7–10.30pm, Wed 7–10.30pm; €€

Again, some 10 minutes' walk away east from the monuments but worth the detour, this well-established *trattoria* is a good place for lunch or an early dinner. It offers a good range of local dishes, including salt cod with leeks, pasta with chick peas and *zuppa pisana*.

€ 3,5

DIRECTORY

Hand-picked hotels and restaurants to suit all budgets and tastes, organised by area, plus select nightlife listings, an alphabetical listing of practical information, a language guide and an overview of the best books and films to give you a flavour of the city.

A suite at the Helvetia & Bristol

ACCOMMODATION

Florence is not a cheap destination when it comes to accommodation, but you definitely get what you pay for. That said, prices can drop considerably outside high season (Christmas, Easter and the summer months), and it is worth asking to see what discounts are available. The city does tend to get booked up very quickly – not surprising considering the high numbers of visitors – so if you have your heart set on a particular place, be sure to book well in advance of your trip.

Places to stay in the city range from sumptuous *palazzi* and boutique hotels to simple but charming B&Bs. Generally, the most expensive hotels are found along the banks of the river with the cheapest accommodation clustered around Santa Maria Novella and San Lorenzo. For a bit of peace and quiet, the villas of Oltrarno and Fiesole are wonderful. If the listings below are fully booked, then the Florence Agenzia per il Turismo website (www.firenzeturismo. it), with its wide array of accommodation, is a useful place to search and make bookings.

Florence introduced a tourist or accommodation tax in 2011. Guests are charged €1.5–5 a night according to the hotel's number of stars. Thus a couple staying four nights in a 4-star hotel would have to pay an extra €36 (payable in cash only). The charge is for a maximum of 7 nights, and children under 12 are exempt.

The Duomo

Brunelleschi
Piazza Santa Elisabetta 3; tel: 055-27370; www.hotelbrunelleschi.it; €€€€
This comfortable four-star hotel is located in a tiny central piazza and partly housed in a church with a 6th-century tower.

Hotel Duomo
Piazza del Duomo 1; tel: 055-219 922; www. hotelduomofirenze.it; €€
This simple and modern hotel is conveniently located in a historic building in the city's main square. Some of the 24 rooms have balconies and enjoy views of the Duomo.

Guelfo Bianco
Via Cavour 29; tel: 055-288 330; www. ilguelfobianco.it; €€
A good option for such a central location, with nicely furnished rooms in two adjacent 15th-century houses just north of the Duomo.

> Price guide for a double room for one night in high season:
> €€€€ = over 300 euros
> €€€ = 150–300 euros
> €€ = 100–150 euros
> € = below 100 euros

Ready to help　　　　　　　　　*Roaring fire at the Helvetia & Bristol*

Relais del Duomo B&B

Piazza dell'Olio 2; tel: 055-210 147; www.
relaisdelduomo.it; €

Just a stone's throw from the Duomo,
the Relais' four rooms are clean and
have a private bath and TV. Can be
noisy at times, but it's a good deal for
Florence, especially during low season.

Piazza della Signoria

Alessandra

Borgo SS Apostoli 17; tel: 055-283 438;
www.hotelalessandra.com; €€

A central *pensione* with rooms ranging
from the quite grand to the more ordinary without bathroom.

Continentale

Vicolo dell'Oro 6r; tel: 055-2726 4000;
www.lungarnocollection.com;
€€€€

Chic retro-style hotel with appealing
designer features, wooden-floored
rooms, comfortable beds and Venetian
blinds. Adding to the mix is top-class
service and a panoramic terrace.

Hermitage

Vicolo Marzio 1, Piazza del Pesce; tel:
055-287 216; www.hermitagehotel.com;
€€€

A delightful hotel located directly above
the Ponte Vecchio, with a lovely roof
garden overlooking the city. Some of
the (rather small) rooms have wonderful river views, although for sleeping you
may prefer to stay in one of the quieter
ones at the back.

Torre Guelfa

Borgo SS Apostoli 8; tel: 055-239 6338;
www.hoteltorreguelfa.com; €€

Part of this hotel includes the tallest privately owned tower (built in 1280) in
Florence. There are pretty furnishings in
bedrooms, and smart bathrooms, but the
winner is the building itself.

Santa Croce

Four Seasons

Borgo Pinti 99; tel: 055-26261; www.
fourseasons.com/florence; €€€€

This superb Renaissance palace was
home to five centuries of Florentine
nobles before its conversion to a hotel
in 2008. Meticulously restored, it
boasts beautiful frescoes, painted ceilings, art-filled bedrooms in silks and
velvet, and sumptuous marble bathrooms. Slightly out of the centre, it has
an 11-acre (4.5-hectare) garden and an
on-site spa. Its restaurant Il Palagio has
a Michelin star.

Grand Cavour

Via del Proconsolo 3; tel: 055-266 271; www.
albergocavour.it; €€€

A luxury hotel in the historic 14th-cen-
tury Palazzo Strozzi-Ridolfi. It is in a quiet
location and has fine city views from the
intimate roof garden. Compared to some
of the other *palazzo* hotels in the city, the
rates here are quite reasonable.

J&J

Via di Mezzo 20; tel: 055-26312; www.
jandjhotel.net; €€€

Room with a garden view at the Regency

Housed in a former convent near Sant' Ambrogio, this smart and discreet hotel has been given a design feel. To add to the style, breakfast is served in the cloister in summer. The rooms are very comfortable; some are enormous.

Locanda Orchidea
Borgo degli Albizi 11; tel: 055-200 1410; www.locandaorchidea.it; €
There are only a handful of rooms in this budget hotel, housed very close to the Duomo, in the 12th-century palazzo in which Dante's wife was born. Furniture is old and quirky, and showers and baths are communal but the place has bags of character and the windows are huge, making the rooms light and airy. Four of the seven rooms overlook a peaceful garden. Closed for most of August.

Plaza Hotel Lucchesi
Lungarno della Zecca Vecchia 38; tel: 055-26236; www.hotelplazalucchesi.it; €€€€
Elegant and friendly hotel overlooking the river (river-view and terraced rooms must be specially requested), a few blocks east of the Uffizi.

Regency
Piazza Massimo d'Azeglio 3; tel: 055-245247; www.regency-hotel.com; €€€€
This is a grand hotel in a 19th-century palazzo, with a highly regarded restaurant and an elegant garden set between the two wings. The rooms are elegant and comfortable with good facilities.

Villa Liana
Via Alfieri 18; tel: 055-245 303; www.hotelliana.com; €€
A quiet, pleasant and slightly faded hotel some way north of the centre in the former British Embassy building. The rooms range from the clean and simple to the elegant 'Count's Room'.

Piazza della Repubblica

Antica Torre di Via Tornabuoni
Via de'Tornabuoni 1; tel: 055-265 8161; www.tornabuoni1.com; €€€
The rooms and apartments here are luxuriously comfortable, and all are set on the 4th, 5th and 6th floors of a medieval palazzo overlooking Piazza Santa Trinità, with bird's-eye views of the city and, from some, the river. *too exp.*

Davanzati
Via Porta Rossa 5; tel: 055-286 666; www.hoteldavanzati.it; €€€ *no avail'lₜ*
In a building dating back to the 1400s, this hotel has been tastefully refurbished and is in a great location.

Firenze
Via del Corso/Piazza Donati 4; tel: 055-268 301; www.hotelfirenze-fi.it; €€
A reasonable hotel with clean rooms whose main advantage is its location. All the rooms have private bathrooms.

Helvetia & Bristol
Via dei Pescioni 2; tel: 055-26651; www.starhotelscollezione.com; €€€€

Regency bathroom

A small but grand hotel, with antiques and paintings scattered around the rooms and hallways. The sumptuous rooms have wonderful views, and the marble-clad bathrooms are a treat. The hotel has a good restaurant and a pretty winter garden.

Savoy
Piazza della Repubblica 7; tel: 055-27351; www.roccofortehotels.com; €€€€
A luxury hotel on the central piazza. Comfortable rooms with contemporary and elegant Italian décor.

Tornabuoni Beacci
Via de'Tornabuoni 3; tel: 055-212 645; www.tornabuonihotels.com; €€€
A lovely hotel set in a 14th-century *palazzo* in the city's most prestigious shopping street. During the first half of 2019 the hotel is closed for refurbishment.

San Lorenzo

Botticelli
Via Taddea 8; tel: 055-290 905; www.hotelbotticelli.it; €€
Located at the back of the central market, this hotel is both comfortable and appealing, with all mod cons alongside original architectural features such as vaulted ceilings and the odd fresco.

Casci
Via Cavour 13; tel: 055-211 686; www.hotelcasci.com; €€
Situated north of the San Lorenzo market area, this frescoed Quattro-cento *palazzo* is family-run, with a welcoming atmosphere. Guest rooms are simply but pleasantly furnished, and look out onto the courtyard, small side streets or gardens.

Centro
Via dei Ginori 17; tel: 055-230 2901; €€
An historic place to stay, near the Via Cavour and the Palazzo Medici-Riccardi. This grand *palazzo* was once Raphael's residence and has now been renovated to provide spacious, light rooms for guests.

Hotel Collodi
Via Taddea 6; tel: 055-291 317; www.hotelcollodi.com; €€
A small, family-run hotel just to the north of San Lorenzo. It is nicely furnished and has some good offers on its rates throughout the year.

Residenza Johanna 1
Via Bonifacio Lupi 14; tel: 055-481 896; www.antichedimorefiorentine.it; €
One of a set of great-value-for-money places to stay in Florence. Set in a residential area to the northwest of the centre, the rooms are comfortable and nicely decorated, but there are few hotel frills.

San Marco

Andrea
Piazza Indipendenza 19; tel: 055-483 890; €€
Situated on a monumental square, this imposing three-star hotel has decent rooms and a great view of the Duomo.

Antica Dimora

Via San Gallo 80/76; tel: 055-462 7296; www.antichedimorefiorentine.it; €€

An excellent-value place to stay (part of a good-value chain), not too far from the centre. The two residences here are set in the area around the church of San Marco. They retain an authentic Tuscan feel and have comfortable, individually decorated rooms.

Cimabue

Via Benifacio Lupi 7; tel: 055-475 601; www.hotelcimabue.it; €

Set in a quiet residential section just outside the centre, this 3-star hotel has a charming setting with hospitable hosts. A leisurely half-hour stroll to the Duomo.

Loggiato dei Serviti

Piazza della Santissima Annunziata 3; tel: 055-289 592; www.loggiatodeiservitihotel.it; €€€

A fabulous place to stay and part of the historic fabric of the city. San Gallo's gracious 16th-century *palazzo* is set on a lovely traffic-free piazza and looks out onto Brunelleschi's Ospedale degli Innocenti. Antiques adorn the vaulted interior, and the rooms are all beautifully decorated.

Morandi alla Crocetta

Via Laura 50; tel: 055-234 4747; www.hotelmorandi.it; €€€

This is a quiet, informal hotel housed in an ex-convent. The 10 peaceful rooms are comfortable and furnished with a few antiques. Several of them have their own private terraces – ask for one of those if the budget allows.

Orto dei Medici

Via San Gallo 30; tel: 055-483 427; www.ortodeimedici.it; €€

This is a small yet imposing palazzo near San Marco. The public rooms have frescoed ceilings, rich in stucco work. Staff are friendly, and the breakfasts are plentiful.

Santa Maria Novella

Albion

Via Il Prato 22r; tel: 055-214 171; www.hotelalbion.it; €€

Set in a stylish neo-gothic *palazzo*, the hotel is a showcase for modern art. The rooms are decent, and free bicycles are available for guests.

Hotel Baglioni

Piazza dell'Unità Italiana 6; tel: 055-23580; www.hotelbaglioni.it; €€€

This classic hotel retains its air of discreet elegance while providing extremely comfortable rooms. The rooftop restaurant has fabulous views of the city skyline. Popular with the business community.

Casa Howard

Via della Scala 18; tel: 06-6992 4555; www.casahoward.com; €€€

A stylish guesthouse, offering upmarket rooms in a fine old mansion; each of the 12 is decorated in a striking individual style, with bold colours contrasting with antiques and old furniture. Great location

Slick décor at J.K. Place

too, next to the Officina di Santa Maria Novella.

Hotel Croce di Malta
Via della Scala 7; tel: 055-261 870; www. crocedimaltaflorence.com; €€€
Conveniently located just off Piazza Santa Maria Novella, near the station, the hotel offers 98 single and double rooms, and 15 exclusive suites.

Grand Hotel Minerva
Piazza Santa Maria Novella 16; tel: 055-27230; www.grandhotelminerva.com; €€€€
One of the few centrally located hotels with a pool, and what's more, it's a rooftop pool with views to die for. Aside from this, the rooms are quietly luxurious and the service is excellent.

J.K. Place
Piazza Santa Maria Novella 7; tel: 055-264 5181; www.jkplace.com; €€€€
This chic and luxurious hotel is tucked into the corner of Piazza Santa Maria Novella. The elegant interiors contain works of art and classic designer furniture and lighting. The suites and penthouse are particularly impressive, and the terrace bar is wonderful.

Mario's
Via Faenza 89; tel: 055-216 801; www. hotelmarios.com; €€
Most of the hotels in Via Faenza near the Mercato Centrale are scruffy, but Mario's is an exception. It's decorated in rustic Tuscan style, with comfortable bedrooms

(the back is quieter) and a pretty breakfast room.

Palazzo dal Borgo
Via della Scala 6; tel: 055-216 237; www. hotelpalazzodalborgo.com; €€€
Formerly the Hotel Aprile, this has been revamped into an elegant four-star hotel. More appealing than most hotels near the station, it is an ex-Medici palace complete with frescoes, a pleasant breakfast room and pretty courtyard.

St Regis
Piazza Ognissanti 1; tel: 055-27161; www. marriott.com; €€€€
In the 5-star St Regis (formerly the Grand) overlooking the Arno, visitors should expect polished service, luxurious guest rooms, gourmet cuisine and fine river views – with prices to match.

Hotel Rivoli
Via della Scala 33; tel: 055-27861; www. hotelrivoli.it; €€€
Conveniently close to Santa Maria Novella, this former Franciscan friary is now a very elegant hotel, with rooms overlooking the former cloisters and an excellent restaurant.

Westin Excelsior
Piazza Ognissanti 3; tel: 055-27151; www. marriott.com; €€€€
Olde-worlde grandeur combined with modern conveniences in this former Florentine address of Napoleon's sister, Caroline; polished service, luxurious rooms

Suite at Villa Cora

and fine views of the Arno from the roof garden. Private parking.

Annalena

Via Romana 34; tel: 055-222 402; www. annalenahotel.com; €€

Great-value antique-furnished rooms in a gracious 15th-century convent that was originally built as a refuge for widows of the Florentine nobility. Located near the Boboli Garden, with views over a pretty garden.

Classic Hotel

Viale Machiavelli 25; tel: 055-229 351; www. classichotel.it; €€

An attractive, pink-washed villa set in a shady garden on a tree-lined avenue just above the Porta Romana.

Lungarno

Borgo San Jacopo 12; tel: 055-27261; www. lungarnocollection.com; €€€€

Smart, comfortable modern hotel popular for its superb position on the river and views of the Ponte Vecchio from the front rooms. There is also a restaurant specialising in fish.

Pitti Palace al Ponte Vecchio

Borgo San Jacopo 3; tel: 055-239 8711; www.florencehotelpittipalacealpontevecchio. com; €€

Small, traditional hotel just south of the Ponte Vecchio contained within the Torre dei Rossi, a tower that dates back to 1200. Private parking.

La Scaletta

Via Guicciardini 13; tel: 055-283 028; www. hotellascaletta.it; €€

Near the Palazzo Pitti, this family-run pensione has an attractive roof garden. The Superior rooms have been refurbished in a contemporary style and have amazing en-suite bathrooms.

Silla

Via de' Renai 5; tel: 055-234 2888; www. hotelsilla.it; €€

An old-fashioned pensione to the southeast of the Ponte Vecchio, overlooking a leafy piazza onto the River Arno. It has a pleasant breakfast terrace.

Torre di Bellosguardo

Via Roti Michelozzi 2; tel: 055-229 8145; www.torrebellosguardo.com; €€€

Set in the hills just above Porta Romana, this quiet, atmospheric and roomy hotel consists of a 14th-century tower attached to a 16th-century villa. It has frescoed reception rooms and charmingly decorated bedrooms, with antiques and quirky details. It has a secluded swimming pool and lovely grounds with a lily pond.

Villa Belvedere

Via Benedetto Castelli 3; tel: 055-222 501; www.villabelvederefirenze.it; €€€

Exceptionally friendly, modern hotel on the hill just above Porta Romana. Sunny rooms, gardens with a swimming pool and tennis court, and lovely views over Florence.

The luxurious Villa San Michele

Villa Cora
Viale Machiavelli 18; tel: 055-228 790; www.
villacora.it; €€€€
This 19th-century villa on the avenue
leading up to Piazzale Michelangelo has
lavish public rooms, extensive gardens,
a heated pool in the park, spa, gym and
gastronomic restaurant.

Hotel Villa La Vedetta
Viale Michelangelo 78; tel: 055-681 631;
www.villalavedettahotel.com; €€€€
Five-star luxury in a neo-Renaissance
villa near the Ponte Vecchio. From the
pool is a panoramic view of the city,
dominated by Brunelleschi's dome.

Fiesole
Pensione Bencistà
Via Benedetto da Maiano 4; tel: 055-59163;
www.bencista.com; €€
Set on the Florence road just south of
Fiesole, this delightful 14th-century villa
lives up to its name, which means 'stay
well'. The grand interior of the sprawling building is full of antiques and rustic furnishings. There are cosy reception
rooms, fine hillside views and, in the
warmer seasons, breakfast is served
alfresco on the lovely terrace. The *pensione* has a spa.

Il Salviatino
Via del Salviatino 21; tel: 055-904 1111; www.
salviatino.com; €€€€
Florence's most luxurious hotel is
housed in a totally restored palatial
15th-century villa in the lush Fiesole

hills, high above the city. Sumptuous
rooms feature 19th century frescoes,
Renaissance art and silver candela-
bras. Guest rooms, including grand
and opulent suites, are all individually furnished. Set in 11 acres of gardens and orchards with infinity pools,
health club, spa and spectacular
views of Florence.

Villa San Michele
Via Doccia 4; tel: 055-567 8200; www.
belmond.com; €€€€
One of the finest and most expensive
hotels in the whole of Tuscany. Sup-
posedly designed by Michelangelo, this
former Franciscan monastery enjoys
harmonious lines and heavenly views of
the city, particularly from the loggia and
restaurant. Spacious grounds.

San Gimignano
L'Antico Pozzo
Via San Matteo 87; tel: 0577-942 014;
www.anticopozzo.com; €€
Old townhouse, carefully restored and
simply but tastefully furnished. Reservations essential.

Siena
Palazzo Ravizza
Pian dei Mantellini 34; tel: 0577-280 462;
www.palazzoravizza.it; €€
Refurbished townhouse with lovely gardens and a good restaurant. Wellchosen
antiques and fabrics in the bedrooms.
The public rooms are welcoming. Half-
board encouraged in summer.

Florentine cheesecake

RESTAURANTS

Dining is an important event in Florence. Once a languid affair, lunch during the working week is increasingly treated as a lighter snack, as more businesses remain open through the lunch hour, and Florentines become more health-conscious. On a Sunday, however, the midday meal is given great importance and may continue well into the afternoon. In the evening, Florentines usually eat at around 8.30pm. Restaurants range from an expensive *ristorante* to a slightly more modestly priced family *trattoria*. Many restaurants still include a cover charge *(coperto)* and some a service *(servizio)* charge of 10–15 percent. If not, leave 10–15 percent for the waiter. Generally speaking the further away from the tourist attractions you go, the less expensive and less touristy the restaurants become. Reservations are recommended for more expensive establishments.

The Duomo

Alle Murate

Via del Proconsolo 16r; tel: 055-240 618;

Price guide for a two-course meal for one with a glass of house wine:
€€€€ = over 60 euros
€€€ = 40–60 euros
€€ = 25–40 euros
€ = below 25 euros

Tue–Sat 11am–midnight; www.fishinglab. it; €€€€

This high-class restaurant is located in a *palazzo* with frescoed vaults. Chef Giovanni Iorio, who has been cooking here for 30 years, offers a creative twist on Tuscan food, using top quality seasonal produce. Reserve.

Coquinarius

Via delle Oche 11r; tel: 055-230 2153; daily 12.30–3pm and 6.30–10.30pm; www. coquinarius.com; €€

This tiny yet fashionable *enoteca* is always full, and has a great selection of wines. You can eat here at almost any time of day. Try the lunch salads, the carpaccio, platters of cheese and cured meats or the rightfully famous pear and pecorino ravioli. Save space for the exquisite homemade desserts.

Piazza della Signoria

Antico Fattore

Via Lambertesca 1/3r; tel: 055-288 975; Mon–Sat noon–3pm, 7–10.30pm; www. anticofattore.it; €€

This traditional *trattoria* offers good meat and game dishes as well as the standard Tuscan and Florentine fare such as *trippa* (tripe) and *ribollita* (vegetable and bread soup).

Cantinetta dei Verrazzano

Via dei Tavolini 18r; tel: 055-268 590;

Lunch at a local ristorante

Piles of tempting nougat

Mon–Sat 8am–4.30pm, Sun 10am–5pm; www.verrazzano.com; €
Popular wine bar serving wines from the family vineyards in Chianti's Castello di Verrazzano. Baked breads from the wood-burning ovens make this a great place to stop for a *merenda* (snack) or light meal, with a dozen Tuscan wines by the glass.

Gustavino
Via della Condotta 37r; tel: 055-239 9806; daily 11am–1pm; www.gustavino. it; €€€
The Tuscan cuisine here is creative without being too elaborate or overfussy, and is served beautifully on large white plates. Look out for the speciality wine-and-food evenings they run. The Canova wine bar next door is open daily (noon–late) for similar dishes, and a choice of over 800 wines, but in a less formal atmosphere. Dinner only Monday to Friday, lunch and dinner Saturday to Sunday.

Oliviero
Via delle Terme 51r; tel: 055-389 6135; daily noon–3pm, 7–11pm; €€€
Historic, sophisticated restaurant that markets itself as being part of the *dolce vita fiorentina* (Florentine good life), this was a former haunt of Liza Minnelli, Sophia Loren and Federico Fellini. The menu changes every couple of months, and everything is prepared freshly in house.

Ora d'Aria
Via dei Georgofili, 11r; tel: 055-200 1619; Tue–Sat 12.30–2.30pm, 7.30–10pm, Mon 7.30–10pm; www.oradariaristorante. com; €€€
Very handy for the Uffizi, this is a fashionable little restaurant renowned for light contemporary variations on classic Tuscan fare, holder of one Michelin star. Reservations recommended (at least 24 hours prior to arrival).

Trattoria del Benvenuto
Via della Mosca 16r; tel: 055-214 833; daily noon–3pm, 7–10.30pm; www. trattoriabenvenuto.it; €€
This offers reasonably priced food in the centre. It is a basic trattoria, but still popular with locals and tourists alike for its welcoming atmosphere.

Vini e Vecchi Sapori
Via dei Magazzini 3r; tel: 055-293 045; Mon–Sat noon–2.30pm, 7–11.30pm; www. vinievecchisapori.it; €€
Tiny, atmospheric trattoria off Piazza della Signoria, this remains a good bet for Tuscan food. The atmosphere manages to retain something of the Florentine, despite the number of tourists who flock to the place.

Santa Croce
Acqua al Due
Via della Vigna Vecchia 40r; tel: 055-284 170; Tue–Sun 7.30–3pm, 7pm–1am, Mon 7pm–1am; www.acquaal2.it; €€

Expect to find excellent grappas in Tuscany

A real dining experience, which requires booking ahead due to its popularity. If you have a big appetite, try the *assaggi di primi* (five pasta dishes chosen by the chef) followed by the *assaggi di dolci* (a selection of the desserts of the day).

Antico Noè
Volta di San Pietro 6r; tel: 055-234 0838; daily 12.30–3pm, 7–10.30pm; www. anticonoe.com; €

Tiny place that offers authentic Tuscan food at low prices as well as 20 different *panini*. The delicious *tagliatelle ai porcini* (mushroom pasta) is recommended.

Baccarossa
Via Ghibellina 58; tel: 055-240 620; Mon–Sat 7pm–midnight; www.baccarossa.it; €€€

A fine restaurant with impeccable food and friendly service. The menu is fish-oriented but meat dishes and vegetarian options are also possible.

La Buchetta
Via dei Benci 3; tel: 055-217 833; daily noon–3pm, 7–11pm; www.labuchetta.com; €€

Known for freshly-made delicious pasta and locally-sourced steaks served at reasonable prices. Staff are very friendly and there is often live music in the evenings.

Caffè and Osteria de' Benci
Via dei Benci 13r; tel: 055-234 4923; daily noon–3pm, 7.30–11pm; €€

A small, relaxed café, where drinks and *panini* are served from the early morning to the late evening, and a next-door *osteria* with more substantial local dishes.

Cantinetta Allegri
Borgo Allegri 58/r; tel: 055-247 8987; daily 11.30am–3pm, 6.30–11.30pm; €€

This Tuscan restaurant is as authentic as it gets, with inexpensive yet incredibly tasty fare served in a simple, cosy setting.

Cantinetta Antinori
Piazza Antinori 3 (off Via de' Tornabuoni); tel: 055-292 234; Mon–Sat noon–2.30pm, 7–10.30pm; www.cantinetta-antinori.com; €€€

Part of the Antinori wine empire and set on the ground floor of Palazzo Antinori, this is an upmarket wine bar with dark wood furnishings and simple Tuscan cuisine. Much of the produce, and the wines of course, come from the Antinori estate.

Le Carceri
Piazza Madonna della Neve 3; tel: 055-247 9327; Tue–Sun noon–3pm, 7pm–midnight, Mon 7pm–midnight; €

A friendly pizzeria, trattoria and wine bar located in the former prison of Le Murate, hence its name.

Il Cibrèo
Via del Verrocchio 8r; tel: 055-234 1100;

Simply prepared pasta

daily 12.50–2.30pm, 6.50–11.15pm;
www.cibreo.com; €€€€
This justly famous restaurant is elegant yet relaxed and one of the most popular with visitors and Florentines alike. The food of chef Fabio Picchi is Tuscan with an innovative twist. Eat much the same food but for a cheaper price in the Cibrèino *trattoria*, which is entered from Piazza Ghiberti.

Cucina Torcicoda
Via Torta 5; tel: 055-265 4329; Mon–Sat 7–10.30pm, Sun noon–2.30pm, 7–10.30pm; www.cucinatorcicoda.com; €€
Hidden in a side street, Cucina Torcicoda has two sections: a restaurant with an extensive menu and a pizza place. Their charcoal-grilled meats are perfection! Good selection of wines. The service is more than excellent.

Enoteca Pinchiorri
Via Ghibellina 87; tel: 055-242 757; Tue–Sat 7.30–10pm; www.enotecapinchiorri.com; €€€€
A foodie's paradise, Enoteca Pinchiorri is garlanded with awards – three Michelin stars no less. Though hailed by some as one of the best restaurants in Europe, it is scorned by others as pretentious. The only way to find out is by taking your credit card and diving in. Offers Tuscan food with a French influence and an outstanding wine list. Booking essential.

Finisterrae
Piazza Santa Croce 12; tel: 055-263 8675; daily 7am–11pm, www.finisterraefirenze.com; €€€
A Mediterranean bar and restaurant with a choice selection of food from various cuisines. Start with tapas, followed by a Moroccan-style *tagine* or pasta dish. The ambience is relaxed and sultry, especially in the bar area.

La Giostra
Borgo Pinti 12r; tel: 055-241 341; Mon–Fri noon–2.30pm, 7pm–1am, Sat–Sun 7pm–1am; www.ristorantelagiostra.com; €€€
This is a renowned restaurant run by a Habsburg prince. The *crostini* are delicious, as are the handmade pasta dishes. White truffles are on offer in season, and they do a mean Wiener Schnitzel and Sacher Torte.

Konnubio
Via dei Conti 8/r; tel: 055-238 1189; daily 7.30am–10.30pm; www.konnubio.it; €€
Located in a cosy, friendly setting, this restaurant has a menu featuring simple yet inventive and beautifully presented dishes. The cuisine here is Tuscan, international and vegan. Another branch is at Corso dei Tintori 10/r.

La Pentola dell'Oro
Via di Mezzo 24/26r; tel: 055-013 9092; Sept–Jul Tue–Sun noon–3pm,

A restaurant at the Savoy Hotel

7–11.30pm; €€€

As well as being unique, this is one of the friendliest restaurants in the city. Chef Giuseppe Alessi is more than willing to explain the dishes, many of which are inspired by medieval and Renaissance Tuscan cuisine.

Il Pizzaiuolo

Via dei Macci 113r; tel: 055-241 171; Mon–Sat 12.30–3pm, 7pm–midnight; www.ilpizzaiuolo.it;
€€

The Neapolitan-style pizzas here are to die for. There are lots more dishes besides if pizza doesn't appeal however, including mixed *antipasti*.

Ristorante del Fagioli

Corso dei Tintori, 47r; tel: 055-244 285; Mon–Fri 12.30–2.30pm, 7.30–10.30pm;
€€

A family style, small eatery serving homemade pastas and beef stew. This restaurant is popular among locals. Come early to avoid waiting for a table. Cash only.

50 Sfumature di Gusto

Via Ghibellina 51/r; tel: 055-245 956; Sun noon–3pm and 7pm–midnight, Mon–Sat 7pm–midnight; €€€

Small but lovely, this establishment serves up exquisite Italian dishes accompanied by complimentary prosecco – what's not to love. Its young chef is wonderfully innovative while the service is keen and attentive.

Il Teatro del Sale

Via dei Macci 111r; tel: 055-200 1492; Tue–Sat 9am–10.30pm, Sun 9am–3pm; www.teatrodelsale.com; €€

Run by the same people as Il Cibreo, this is a unique three-meal-a-day restaurant and theatre all in one. Fabio Picchi produces Tuscan dishes, buffet-style, on the theatre stage. Reservations are required for this novel experience. Fixed price for dinner plus a small fee for theatre membership.

Piazza della Repubblica

Chiaro Scuro

Via del Corso 36r; tel: 055-214 247; daily 7.30am–9.30pm; www.chiaroscuro.it; €

This café has coffee from all over the world, as well as flavoured hot chocolates, cocktails, a buffet lunch and one of the best *aperitivo* buffets in Florence.

Irene (The Savoy)

Piazza della Repubblica 7; tel: 055-273 5891; daily 7–11am, 12.30–3.30pm, 7.30–8.30pm; www.roccofortehotels.com; €€€€

The Savoy's bar and restaurant makes for an elegant setting in which to enjoy Tuscan cuisine from a select menu. Not cheap, but the food is delicious and the service excellent.

Il Paiolo

Via del Corso 42r; tel: 055-215 019; daily 11am–11pm; www.ristoranteilpaiolo.it;
€€

Tiramisu with a twist

A cosy restaurant that serves good-quality pan-Italian food. The fresh fish and homemade desserts are the highlights.

Perché No?
Via de' Tavolini 19r; tel: 055-239 8969; Wed–Mon and Wed–Fri 11am–10pm; €
One of the oldest ice cream parlours in town and a pioneer of the *semifreddo* – a mousse-like *gelato* that is perfect for colder days.

San Lorenzo

Giannino in San Lorenzo
Borgo San Lorenzo 35/37r; tel: 055-239 9799; daily 11am–11.30pm; www.gianninoinflorence.com; €€
One of the better restaurants in this area, offering traditional food such as *bistecca alla fiorentina* and *ribollita* and a good wine selection. Special themed evenings are worth looking out for.

Lobs
Via Faenza 75r; tel: 055-212 478; Tue–Sun noon–2.30pm and 6.30–10.30pm; €€€
One of the best fish restaurants in Florence, Lobs offers a range of seafood including swordfish, prawns, octopus and oysters. The lobster should be ordered in advance.

Nerbone
Piazza del Mercato Centrale, inside the market; tel: 055-219 949; Mon–Sat 8am–3pm; €

One of the most popular lunch spots in the area, Nerbone serves up a daily menu with local dishes featuring seasonal ingredients. The bollito sandwich, with boiled meat, is a favourite. Lunch only Monday to Saturday.

Osteria dell'Agnolo
Borgo San Lorenzo 24r; tel: 055-285 923; daily 11am–midnight; www.osteriadellagnolo.it; €€
Home-made pasta and a range of pizzas, *calzoni* and desserts make this *osteria* a good, solid, albeit touristy, option near the market.

Trattoria ZàZà
Piazza del Mercato Centrale 26r; tel: 055-215 411; daily 11am–11pm; www.trattoriazaza.it; €€€
Set in the piazza behind the market, this lively taverna-like *trattoria* offers pizzas and pasta, meat and fish-based dishes, and a good choice of wines.

San Marco

Pugi
Piazza San Marco 9b; tel: 055-280 981; Mon–Sat 7.45am–8pm; www.fornopugi.it; €
Famous among Florentines for its *schiacciate* (flat breads of various kinds). Buy focaccia or pizza by weight as a snack or for lunch on the run.

Ristorante da Mimmo
Via San Gallo 57/59r; tel: 055-481 030; Mon–Fri noon–2.30pm, 6.30–11pm, Sat

Serving up spaghetti carbonara

6.30–11pm; www.ristorantedamimmo.it; €€

Located within a former theatre, this place offers good food and wine at affordable prices. There's a changing menu, which is often inspired by southern Italian cooking.

Taverna del Bronzino

Via delle Ruote 27r; tel: 055-495 220; Mon–Fri 12.30–2.30pm, 7.30–10.30pm; www.tavernadelbronzino.net; €€€€

A variety of European cuisines served in an elegant restaurant with a vaulted ceiling and patio. Try the *ravioli alla senese* (ricotta-and-spinach-filled pasta) or one of the less Italian but equally divine dishes.

Il Vegetariano

Via delle Ruote 30r; tel: 055-475 030; Mon 12.30–2.30pm, Tue–Fri 12.30–2.30pm, 7.30–10.30pm, Sat–Sun 7.30–10.30pm; www.il-vegetariano.com; €

This restaurant's use of the freshest vegetables in its selection of dishes makes it a strong contender for the city's best vegetarian eatery, although admittedly there aren't that many to choose from in Florence. Informal and unassuming.

Santa Maria Novella

Benedicta

Hotel Rivoli, Via della Scala 33/ Via Benedetta 12r; tel: 055-264 5429; Mon–Sat 7.30–11pm; www.ristorantebenedicta.it; €€

Dependable Tuscan dishes with a creative twist, ranging from steak to pasta, are served here in a contemporary setting which is at odds with the building's former occupation as a Franciscan convent.

Buca Lapi

Via del Trebbio 1r; tel: 055-213 768; Mon–Sat 7–10.30pm; www.bucalapi.com; €€€

In the cellar of the Palazzo Antinori, this lovely restaurant is regarded as serving one of the best *bistecca alla fiorentina* (enormous and beautifully grilled). As expected, being in the basement of the *palazzo* of one of Tuscany's best wine producers, it has an excellent range of wines.

Coco Lezzone

Via del Parioncino 26/r; tel: 055-287 178; Mon–Sat noon–2.15pm, 7–10.15pm; closed Tue evening; www.cocolezzone.it; €€

A small, popular, no-frills institution off the elite shopping strip Via Tornabuoni, serving classic Florentine food on small tables with red and white checked cloths. Try the tasty pasta with porcini mushrooms. No credit cards.

Harry's Bar

Lungarno A. Vespucci 22r; tel: 055-239 6700; daily noon–2.30pm, 7–11pm; www.harrysbarfirenze.com; €€€€

Rustic oven–baked pizza   *Tuscan stew*

Modelled on the original in Venice made famous by Ernest Hemingway, Harry's is an American-style restaurant and bar. It is renowned more for its cocktails than its food, but the latter is often innovative, and fish figures largely on the menu.

Il Latini
Via del Palchetti 6r; tel: 055-210 916; Tue–Fri 7.30–10.30pm, Sat–Sun 12.30–2.30pm, 7.30–10.30pm; www.illatini.com; €€
Expect to queue to get into this sprawling noisy eatery with communal tables. The Tuscan food is good and filling, and the ambience is convivial and fun.

La Carabaccia
Via Palazzuolo 190r; tel: 055-214 782; Thu–Tue noon–2.45pm, 7–11pm; www.trattorialacarabaccia.com; €€€
Set in a renovated old tavern, La Carabaccia offers a daily and seasonal menu using the freshest ingredients. The specialities include grilled meats cooked on charcoal and traditional Tuscan dishes. The excellent food is supplemented by a stone cellar full of the best Tuscan wines – they also make their own basil liqueur. The setting is a medieval Florentine dining room, complete with original features.

Ruth's
Via Luigi Carlo Farini 2a; tel: 055-248 0888; Sun–Thu noon– 2.30pm, 7–10pm, Fri noon–3pm, Sat 7–10pm; www.kosheruth.com; €
Next to the grand synagogue, this little place is one of the few to cater for vegetarians. It offers a range of kosher and Middle Eastern-style dishes from falafel to couscous and hummus.

Trattoria Sostanza
Via del Porcellana 25r; tel: 055-212 691; Mon–Fri 12.30–2pm, 7.30–9.45pm; €€
Relaxed restaurant with basic decor and communal seating, offering traditional Tuscan dishes including *tortellini in brodo* (*tortellini* in broth). Concessions are not made for tourists, and some basic Italian would be useful. However, this is a true Florentine dining experience: substantial and satisfying food. No credit cards.

Oltrarno

Antica Mescita San Niccolò
Via di San Niccolò 60r, tel: 055-234 2836; daily noon–12.30am; www.osteriasanniccolo.webnode.it; €
This osteria in Oltrarno does simple and cheap, but extremely good Italian food served up in a cheery, crowded atmosphere. Part of the eatery is set in a former chapel.

Antico Ristoro di' Cambi
Via Sant' Onofrio 1r; tel: 055-217 134; Mon–Sat noon–2.30pm, 6–10.30pm; www.anticoristorodicambi.it; €

Lunch during the Palio in Siena

This popular restaurant fits perfectly into the heart of the bustling San Frediano area. Traditional in feel and food, it offers excellent Tuscan cooking and no-nonsense service.

Bevo Vino
Via di San Niccolò 59r; tel: 055-200 1709; daily noon–midnight; €

A lovely medium-sized *enoteca*, offering daily specials for first and second courses, plus carpaccio and bruschetta. Good wine and cheese selections, and the service is friendly and knowledgeable. Outdoor seating is available in the summer.

Filipepe
Via di San Niccolò 39r; tel: 055-200 1397; Mon–Sat 7.30–11pm; €€€

Filipepe offers an elegant take on modern Mediterranean cuisine. Soft candle lighting, cove ceilings, and the bottles of wine lining the walls give each area a private yet comfortable feel. The menu offers a seasonal selection of ingredients, frequently from the southern regions of Italy, including different kinds of carpaccio, salads, soups and pastas. There is a small outdoor area for meals in summer.

Osteria del Cinghiale Bianco
Borgo S. Jacopo 43/r; tel: 055-215 706; daily 6.30–10.30pm, Sat–Sun also noon–2.30pm; www.cinghialebianco.com; €€

Traditional dishes including hard-to-find cinghiale (wild boar) are even tastier in the medieval, mood-setting ambience accented by a few romantic niche tables. If cinghiale is not for you, there is a wide selection of simple classic Tuscan fare.

Pitti Gola e Cantina
Piazza de' Pitti 16; tel: 055-212 704; Wed–Mon noon–11pm; www.pittigolaecantina.com; €

This is a great little enoteca, lined with shelving containing innumerable bottles of wine, many available by the glass. Pasta dishes and simple but tasty plates of *salumi* and cheese help the wine slip down.

Quattro Leoni
Piazza della Passera, Via de' Vellutini 1r; tel: 055-218 562; daily noon–midnight; www.4leoni.com; €€

One of the city's oldest restaurants, founded in 1550, this eatery is in a quiet square where diners can sit outside during the summer. The traditional cooking is excellent and there are new additions to the Tuscan menu on a daily basis.

Rifrullo
Via di San Niccolo 55r; tel: 055-234 2621; Mon–Thu 7.30am–12.30am, Fri until 2am, Sat 8.30am–2pm, Sun 8am–12.30am; www.ilrifrullo.com; €€

This hip hang-out is a café by day, serving morning pastries and coffee, then tasty pasta for lunch. By night, it is a popular *aperitivo* locale, offering

Caffè Boboli in San Gimignano

drinks and a plentiful buffet. Rifrullo also offers an evening menu and a garden for alfresco meals.

Sant' Agostino 23
Via Sant' Agostino 23r; tel: 055-281 995; daily noon–11pm; €€
Trattoria between Santo Spirito and the Brancacci Chapel, combining Tuscan staples (osso bucco and *ribollita*) with simple international fare. The emphasis is on fresh ingredients.

Outside Florence
Ristorante La Reggia Degli Etruschi
Via S. Francesco, 18; tel: 055-59385; daily 12.30–2pm, 7–10pm; www.lareggiadeglietruschi.com; €€
A little out of town but beautifully located on a hill in Fiesole. This restaurant offers elegantly served traditional Tuscan food accompanied by jazz or classical music as well as enchanting, panoramic views, especially at sunset.

San Gimignano
Dorandò
Vicolo dell'Oro 2; tel: 0577-941 862; daily noon–2.30pm, 7–9.30pm, closed Mon Dec–Easter; www.ristorantedorando.it; €€€
The Dorandò's local dishes are beautifully prepared and meticulously researched, as one of their aims is to preserve the traditions of the village. This is one of the best restaurants in San Gimignano, so be sure to book ahead.

Siena
La Taverna di San Giuseppe
Via Giovanni Duprè 132; tel: 0577-42286; Mon–Sat noon–2.30pm, 7–10pm; www.tavernasangiuseppe.it; €€€
An outstanding restaurant known, above all, for its delicious pasta with truffles and excellent wines from the restaurant's Etruscan cellar. Exceptional service and an amazing, warm atmosphere.

Osteria del Castelvecchio
Via Castelvecchio 65; tel: 0577-47093; daily noon–2.45pm, 7–10.45pm; €€
Converted from ancient stables, this lovely informal *osteria* serves traditional and often lesser-known Sienese dishes. There are good daily choices for vegetarians and lots of excellent meat dishes, plus an interesting wine list. Opening times tend to change, so check when you book.

Osteria Le Logge
Via del Porrione 33; tel: 0577-48013; Mon–Sat noon–2.45pm and 7–10.45pm; www.osterialelogge.it; €€€
This restaurant, founded by the late Gianni Brunelli and his wife, is set in a delightful location: a 19th-century grocer's shop with an authentic dark-wood, vaulted ceiling and marble interior. The menu is likely to offer duck and fennel pasta with black truffles and stuffed guinea fowl (*faraona*).

Teatro Goldoni

NIGHTLIFE

In Florence the main theatres listed below not only put on seasons of music, opera and dance but also plays, generally in Italian, and other events throughout the year. For many visitors nightlife amounts to no more than a meal out, a stroll through the floodlit centre and a drink or two to end off the evening. Florence is not renowned for nightclubs but has a good number of bars, often with live music. Classical concerts are held in churches year-round, and in summer piazzas are the stage for a variety of performers, classical and contemporary.

Fiesole's Roman Amphitheatre (Teatro Romano) features heavily in the town's annual summer festival, Estate Fiesolana (June and July), when it is used to stage open-air performances of concerts, ballet, drama and film. See www.bitconcerti.it for further information.

Theatre

Opera di Firenze/Maggio Musicale Fiorentino
Piazzale Vittorio Gui 1; tel: 055-277 9309;
www.maggiofiorentino.com
The main theatre for the Maggio Musicale festival, the Opera di Firenze also puts on a full programme of concerts, operas and other events year round (book online or in person at the box office).

Teatro Goldoni
Via Santa Maria 15; tel: 055-277 9350

This small, attractive 18th-century theatre in Oltrarno is used for some performances during the Maggio as well as shows for the Florence Dance Festival (www.florencedancefestival.org).

Teatro Niccolini
Via Ricasoli 3; tel: 055-094 6404; www.teatroniccolini.com
Florence's oldest theatre (1650), restored to its full glory, reopened after a 20-year closure in January 2016.

Teatro della Pergola
Via della Pergola 18–32; tel: 055-22641; www.teatrodellapergola.com
This beautiful 17th-century theatre hosts a world-class chamber music season organised by the Amici della Musica (www.amicimusicafirenze.it) as well as plays by noted Italian companies, chamber concerts and some opera.

Teatro Puccini
Via delle Cascine 41; tel: 055-362 067; www.teatropuccini.it
This theatre on the outskirts of town once served as a cinema but now hosts seasons of plays as well as the occasional opera. Built in 1939–40, it is one of the most impressive examples of Fascist-era architecture in the city.

Teatro del Sale
Via dei Macci 111; tel: 055-200 1492;

Sipping cocktails at Dolce Vita

restaurant Tue–Sat 9am–10.30pm, Sun until 3pm; www.teatrodelsale.com
This old theatre northeast of Santa Croce provides a novel experience, combining theatre with dinner. Fabio Picchi (of the Cibrèo emporium, see page 112) produces Tuscan dishes, buffet-style on the theatre stage. The tables are then taken away and the show begins. The dinner is a fixed affordable price, with a small fee for the theatre membership. Reservations are required.

Teatro Verdi

Via Ghibellina 99; tel: 055-212 320; www. teatroverdifirenze.it
The vast Teatro Verdi is the venue for light opera, ballet, jazz and rock concerts. The Orchestra Regionale Toscana's lively concert series is held here and runs from December to May.

Cinema

Odeon

Piazza Strozzi 2; tel: 055-214 068; www. odeonfirenze.com
Just west of Piazza della Repubblica, this is one of the few cinemas in Florence that regularly shows films in their original language. Films in English are shown on what is known as 'Odeon Original Sound nights' (check the website for details). At other times the programme includes a mix of Italian and dubbed films.

Bars and live music

Dolce Vita

Piazza del Carmine; tel: 055-284 595; http://new.dolcevitafirenze.it
This fashionable, arty bar-club in the Oltrarno quarter draws the crowds during happy hour and for after dinner drinks. *Aperitivi* come with a generous buffet and you can sit outside at tables overlooking Carmine church. Live music three times a week from 8pm–10pm, followed by a DJ until the early hours of the morning.

Ganzo

Via dei Macci 85r; tel: 055-241 076; www. ganzoflorence.it
Ganzo is Tuscan for 'cool' and this is a bar and club for the arts, with lectures, exhibitions and culinary events.

Moyo

Via dei Benci 23r; tel: 055-247 9738; www. moyo.it
This swanky cocktail bar in the Santa Croce area offers a good buffet for the price of your cocktail (buffet served 7–10.30pm, with dancing later). Weekly themes might include a sushi buffet or Mexico *aperitivo* and Latin party. It is open all day for drinks and light meals, and has free Wi-Fi.

Zoe

Via de Renai 13r; tel: 055-243 111; www. zoebar.it
This is a popular and stylish spot for summer evening cocktails, with an aperitif buffet and DJ music. It's also open throughout the day for snacks and light meals.

Piazza della Repubblica carousel

A–Z

A

Age restrictions

The age of consent for heterosexual, gay and lesbian sex is 14. You must be 18 to drive and 16 to buy alcohol.

Addresses

If the letter 'r' appears after numbers in an address, it refers to *rosso* (red) and denotes a business address; Florentine addresses operate a dual numbering system, with 'red' numbers usually denoting businesses and blue or black numbers usually denoting residential addresses.

B

Budgeting

Florence is relatively expensive in terms of accommodation with little under €100 per night at the budget end of things, and the sky being the limit for the luxury hotels. Depending on what wine you choose, a glass will cost around €4–6. Allow €25–40 per head for an evening meal.

A standard bus fare is €1.20 for 90 minutes of travel. A 24-hour ticket is €5, and a three-day pass costs €12.

The Firenze Card is a museum pass (€85) which is valid for 72 hours and allows admission to 76 museums (including the famous ones) in Florence.

The Firenzecard+ (€92) allows unlimited access to the city's public transport in addition to the museums. This represents good value for keen sightseers and it means skipping the queues, but if you are just visiting a couple of museums, it is not worth the outlay. Under the Martedì in Arte initiative the major state museums are free to the public from 7–11pm on the last Tuesday of every month.

C

Carbon off-setting

Air travel produces a huge amount of carbon dioxide and is a significant contributor to climate change. If you would like to off-set the damage caused to the environment by your flight, a number of organisations can do this for you, using on-line 'carbon calculators', which tell you how much you need to donate. In the UK travellers can visit www.climate-care.org; in the US log on to www.climatefriendly.com.

Children

At first sight, art and architecture-heavy Florence may not appear to be the best place to take children, but there are some museums and other sights that hold some appeal (such as climbing the dome of the Duomo or the mummies in the Museo Archaeologico). The Boboli Garden and the Cascine are Florence's two main parks, where kids can let off steam, while one of the few children's playgrounds is to be found in Piazza dell'Azeglio. Italians are very fond and tolerant of children, and finding a restaurant to eat with them should not be a problem. Florence also has numerous ice cream parlours, which should be popular with kids.

Climate

The climate in Florence can be extreme. Its position, lying in a bowl surrounded by hills, accounts for the high degree of humidity that is often a feature of the weather in midsummer. The heat and humidity are generally at their most intense between mid-July and mid-August, when temperatures frequently climb into the 30s Celsius (high 90s Fahrenheit). Winters can be very cold and damp, but there are a good number of cold, crisp and sunny days, and visiting the city at this time of year, without the crowds, can be very pleasant.

The city seems to get more and more crowded each year, the peak periods being around Easter time and from June to the end of August. The only relatively tourist-free months are November to February. The best months to visit are May, September and early October, when the temperatures are pleasantly warm but not too hot for sightseeing.

Clothing

Casual wear is acceptable in all but the grandest restaurants. Clothing should be as light as possible for summer, but take a jumper for the evenings, which can be surprisingly cool. If you go in spring or autumn, it is worth taking a light raincoat or umbrella. In winter (Nov– Mar), the temperature frequently drops to freezing or below, and warm clothing is essential. A pair of comfortable shoes is invaluable for sightseeing and walking the cobbled streets. Shorts and bare shoulders are frowned upon and frequently forbidden in churches.

Crime and safety

While Florence is generally a safe city, petty crime is a major problem, particularly pick-pocketing and the snatching of handbags and jewellery in the street and on buses. One popular scam is for someone to approach you to distract your attention while someone else steals your purse or wallet. Keep your valuables hidden on your person and your hand on your bag to help avoid this. Make sure you report any thefts to the police, since you will need evidence of the crime in the form of a police report to claim insurance.

Customs and duty-free

It is no longer possible to buy duty-free or tax-free goods on journeys within the European Union (EU). VAT and duty are included in the purchase price. Shops at ports and airport terminals will sell goods duty- and tax-paid to those travelling within the EU; they may choose not to pass on price increases. Airports

Elaborate carved stonework

can have separate duty-free shops for those travelling outside the EU or single shops selling duty-free goods alongside duty/tax-paid goods.

Since the sale of duty-free goods in any EU country has been abolished, there are no longer any limits on how much you can buy on journeys within the EU, provided it is for your own personal use. However, there are certain suggested limits, and if you exceed them, the customs department may seize your goods if you cannot prove they are for your own use. The guidance levels are 800 cigarettes or 400 cigarillos or 200 cigars or 1kg of smoking tobacco; 10 litres of spirits; 20 litres of fortified wine; 90 litres of wine; 110 litres of beer. Duty-free is still available to those travelling outside the EU.

D

Disabled travellers

Despite difficult cobbled streets and poor wheelchair access to tourist attractions and hotels, many people with disabilities visit Florence and Tuscany every year. Unaccompanied visitors will usually experience some difficulty, so it is best to travel with a companion. Specialised tour operators or travel agencies offering customised tours and itineraries for those with disabilities include Flying Wheels Travel (www.flyingwheelstravel.com) and Accessible Journeys (www.accessiblejourneys.com). Access-Able Travel Source (www.

access-abletravel.com.au) is a database of travel agents from around the world with experience in accessible travel. In the UK you can obtain further information from Disability Rights UK (www.disabilityrightsuk.org) and in the US from SATH (www.sath.org).

#

Electricity

Italy uses 220v and two-pin plugs, for which you will need an adaptor.

Embassies and consulates

Australian Embassy: Via Antonio Bosio 5, 00161 Rome; tel: 06-852 721.
UK Embassy: Via XX Settembre 80a, 00187 Rome; tel: 06-4220 0001.
UK Consulate: Lungarno Corsini 2, 50123 Florence; tel: 055-284 133.
US Embassy: Via Vittorio Veneto 121, 00187 Rome; tel: 06-46741.
US Consulate: Lungarno A. Vespucci 38, 50123 Florence; tel: 055-266 951.

Emergencies

The European Emergency Number: 112
Police (Carabinieri): 112
Police (Polizia): 113
Fire Brigade (Vigili del Fuoco): 115
Ambulance (Misericordia): 118
Municipal Police: tel: 055-328 3333

Etiquette

Italians tend to be friendly, but will have no qualms about showing their dis-

A second-hand booksellers

pleasure should you do something to offend them. Being polite and trying to speak a little Italian goes a long way. Both men and women greet each other with a kiss on each cheek.

F

Festivals

Easter Day: *Scoppio del Carro*, the Explosion of the Cart (actually fireworks on a float). An ancient ritual accompanied by processions of musicians and flag-throwers in Renaissance costume, starting at the Porta a Prato and ending at Piazza del Duomo.

Ascension Day: *Festa del Grillo*, Festival of the Crickets, in Parco delle Cascine. Children used to bring or buy crickets in cages, but the insects have now been replaced by toy versions. There's also a large general market.

May and June: *Maggio Musicale Fiorentino*. A festival comprising opera, ballet, concerts and recitals. It closes with two free concerts held in the Piazza della Signoria.

16–17 June: *Luminaria di San Ranieri* (Pisa). A spectacular event, with thousands of candles lit on the buildings along the Arno. A boat race takes place on the second day.

24 June: *San Giovanni*. Florence's patron saint's day and a public holiday in the city. The *calcio* in costume football game is played in Piazza Santa Croce; other matches are also played around this time.

Last Sunday in June: *Il Gioco del Ponte* (Pisa). A kind of medieval tug-of-war played out on the Ponte di Mezzo.

2 July and 16 August: Palio horse races (Siena). The famous horse races take place on these two dates.

July: *Florence Dance Festival*. A three-week festival of dance at outdoor venues in Florence.

G

Green issues

The last two mayors of Florence have given high priority to eco-friendly transport, reducing smog and preserving green areas of the city. The first move was to ban all vehicles from the city centre which will substantially reduce the carbon monoxide and fine particulate that was suffocating the city centre – and sullying the Duomo. Small electric buses weave their way around the periphery, and there are an increasing number of bike lanes. However, outlying streets are clogged with traffic and you will see many cars parked on pavements.

Guides and tours

For art and history tours contact AGT FLorence (www.florenceguidesagt.com) or ArtViva (www. artviva.com).

Some travel agencies and bus companies offer organised bus tours of the countryside around Florence, including excursions to San Gimignano/Siena or Pisa. Details can be obtained through your hotel, tourist information offices and local travel agencies.

H

Health

Insurance

EU residents are entitled to the same medical treatment as an Italian citizen. Visitors will need to get an EHIC card (see www.nhs.uk for information) before they go. This covers medical treatment and medicines, although it is still necessary to pay prescription charges and a percentage of the costs for medicines. Note that the EHIC does not give any cover for trip cancellations, nor does it provide repatriation in case of illness. For this, you will need to take out private insurance. However, when the UK leaves the EU this could change. Canadian citizens are also covered by a reciprocal arrangement between the Italian and Canadian governments. US citizens, however, are strongly advised to take out private insurance.

If you are covered by a reciprocal scheme and need to visit a doctor while in Italy, take the EHIC card (if an EU resident) or proof of citizenship and residence (eg passport) to the local health office (Unità Sanitaria Locale), which will direct you to a doctor covered by the state system and supply the necessary paperwork.

Pharmacies and hospitals

Pharmacies: the staff in chemists' shops *(farmacie)* are usually very knowl-edgeable about common illnesses and sell far more medicines without prescription than their colleagues in other Western countries.

Every *farmacia* has a list of the local pharmacies which are open at night and on Sundays.

Chemists' shops that are open 24 hours *(farmacie aperte 24 ore su 24)* in Florence are:

Farmacia all'Insegna del Moro, Piazza San Giovanni 20/r; tel: 055-211 343

Farmacia Comunale, Santa Maria Novella Station; tel: 055-216 761.

Farmazia Molteni, Via Calzaiouli 7/r; tel: 055-215 472

There is an accident and emergency department in the city centre at Ospedale Santa Maria Nuova, Piazza Santa Maria Nuova 1; tel: 055-69381.

Hours and holidays

Business hours

Offices are usually open from 8am–1pm and from 2–4pm, though many now stay open all day. Normal banking hours are Mon–Fri 8.30am–noon/1pm and 2.30–4.30pm. On national holidays, all shops, offices and schools are closed. Standard shop opening times are Mon–Sat 8.30/9am to 1/1.30pm and 3.30/4pm to 7.30/8pm but an increasing number of shops are open all day.

Public holidays

The dates of the national holidays in Florence are:

1 Jan *Capodanno* (New Year's Day)
6 Jan *La Befana* (Epiphany)
Easter *Pasqua*
Easter Monday *Pasquetta*
25 Apr *Anniversario della Liberazione* (Liberation Day)
1 May *Festa del Lavoro* (Workers' Day)
2 June *Festa della Repubblica* (Republic Day)
24 June *San Giovanni* (St John the Baptist, Florence's patron saint)
15 Aug *Ferragosti* (Assumption of the Blessed Virgin Mary)
1 Nov *Tutti Santi* (All Saints' Day)
8 Dec *Immacolata Concezione* (Immaculate Conception)
25 Dec *Natale* (Christmas)
26 Dec *Santo Stefano* (Boxing Day)

I

Internet

Most large hotels offer internet access and Wi-Fi. The Florence Wi-Fi initiative provides free internet access in several locations around the city. The 72-hour Firenze Card comes with 72 hours of free Wi-Fi at a number of hubs in central Florence.

L

Left luggage

Left-luggage facilities can be found at Santa Maria Novella railway station.

LGBTQ travellers

Florence is an easy-going destination for gay and lesbian visitors, with a lively local scene helped by the presence of many students and the Florentines' generally liberal outlook on life. The national LGBT organisation Arcigay (tel: 051-095 7241; www.arcigay.it) has an active branch in the city (Via di Mezzo 39r) that can provide help and information. Their website (partly in Italian) features useful information on local activism and events.

M

Maps

Tourist offices can supply free maps of the city centre and also have a useful map on their website (www.firenzeturismo.it). One of the best commercially available maps of the city is by the Touring Club Italiano and is available in bookshops and at newsstands.

Media

Print

La Stampa, *Il Corriere della Sera* and *La Repubblica* are national papers with local sections, while the gossipy *La Nazione* is the region's paper favoured by most Florentines for its coverage of local news. English-language freebies include the fortnightly *The Florentine* (www.theflorentine.net) with excellent articles on Florence, Tuscany and Italy. *Firenze Spettacolo* (www.firenzespettacolo.it) available from all newsstands, is the most informative monthly listings magazine.

Sienese architecture

Television and radio

Television is deregulated in Italy. The Italian state TV network, RAI, broadcasts three channels which compete with various independent channels. There is also a vast number of radio stations, including many regional ones. Satellite gives access to CNN and BBC World in many hotels.

Money

In common with the other Eurozone countries of the EU, Italy's monetary unit is the euro (€), which is divided into 100 cents. Bank notes are issued in denominations of 5, 10, 20, 50, 100, 200 and 500 euros. Coins are denominated in 1 and 2 euros, and 1, 2, 5, 10, 20 and 50 cents.

Credit cards

Most major credit cards, including Visa, American Express and MasterCard, are accepted in hotels, restaurants and shops, for air and train tickets, and for cash in any bank and some ATMs.

Banks, exchange and ATMs

Changing money in a bank can be time-consuming, but the rates are generally better than in exchange offices. Exchange offices are found all over Florence, and at the train station.

P

Police

Italy has different types of police: the armed paramilitary *Carabinieri* who deal with serious violent crime and the state and municipal police who are responsible for day-to-day policing (including traffic). For emergencies, see page 124.

Post

The main post office in Florence is in Via Pellicceria 3 (near Piazza della Repubblica; www.poste.it), open Mon–Fri 8.30am–7.05pm and Sat 8.15am–12.30pm. There are local post offices in each area of the city, generally open Mon–Fri 8.15am–1.30pm and Sat 8.15am–12.30pm (or closed on Sat).

Stamps *(francobolli)* are sold at post offices and tobacconists' shops *(tabacchi)*.

R

Religion

Although it has no official state religion, Italy is an overwhelmingly Catholic country, and the ideals and influence of the Vatican permeate Italian life and politics. While Tuscany is generally tolerant and accepting of other religions, religious and racial intolerance, especially against Roma and Muslims, is a growing problem in Italy, fomented by political parties such as the Lega Nord and Alleanza Nazionale.

S

Smoking

Smoking in enclosed public places is banned in Italy. The law is widely obeyed

Neptune fountain

and hefty fines are given out to those who flaunt it.

Sports

Gyms
Klab
Tel: 055-708 787; www.klab.it
Two fitness centres in Florence, which also run a number of classes.
Palestra Ricciardi
Borgo Pinti 75; tel: 055-247 8444; www.palestraricciardi.it
A central gym where staff speak good English as well as some French and Spanish.
Tropos
Via Orcagna 20a; tel: 055-678 381; www.troposfirenze.it
A luxurious, and pricey, fitness and beauty centre with gym and swimming pool.

Tennis
Circolo Carraia
Via Monti alle Croci, Florence; tel: 055-234 6353; www.tenniscarraia.it (booking of the fields reserved to the members of the club)
Circolo del Tennis
Parco delle Cascine; tel: 055-332 651; www.ctfirenze.it

Swimming
Many luxury hotels outside the centre of Florence have swimming pools which may allow guests for a small fee. There are also public pools in towns – although these have erratic opening hours and can be by subscription only. The following swimming pools are in Florence:
Piscina Comunale Bellariva
Lungarno Aldo Moro 6; tel: 055-626 6007
Open-air during the summer.
Piscina Costoli
Viale Paoli, Campo di Marte; tel: 055-623 6027
This is in the north of the city and has a clean outdoor pool in the summer.
Piscina Le Pavoniere
Via Catena 2; tel: 392 172 4859
Set in the Parco delle Cascine and only open in summer, this is one of the city's most appealing pools.

Football
The main spectator sport in Tuscany is football. Florentines are football fanatics and passionate supporters of the local team 'La Fiorentina'. They play regularly at the Stadio Artemio Franchi (tel: 055-503 011), and the season runs on Sundays from August to May, with games in the afternoon or the evening.

Next to the stadium is the athletics arena, which also hosts a number of events during the year. The Firenze Marathon takes place annually – www.firenzemarathon.it.

Student travellers

State-run museums are free for EU citizens under 18 and half-price for those aged between 18–25 years (passport or driver's license required). An ISIC

(International Student Identity Card) or IYTC (International Youth Travel Card) can be useful for discounts on shops and entertainment, and occasionally for accommodation and eating out. For details go to www.isic.org.

Strikes

Italy has active trade unions, and strikes are frequent, causing disruptions to transport and other services. Strikes are usually publicised in advance on posters or in newspapers.

T

Telephones

Italy has a decreasing number of telephone kiosks, but almost every bar has a public phone. Telephone cards (*schede telefoniche*) – both Telecom Italia and other ones – can be purchased from tobacconists (*tabacchi*), newsstands and other shops with the appropriate sticker in the window.

The international dialling code for Italy is 39, and the code for Florence is 055. Note that when calling from abroad you retain the initial zero on the local code. To call abroad from Italy, dial 00, then the country code (61 for Australia, 1 for Canada and the US, 353 for Ireland, 64 for New Zealand and 44 for the UK).

Mobile phones

In 2017 the EU introduced a new regulation abolishing roaming charges in the EU. The charges will not after Brexit; the regulations on mobile roaming will apply until at least 31 December 2020. If your phone is 'unlocked' (contact your provider for details), it is straightforward to buy a local pay-as-you-go SIM card. The main providers are Vodafone Italia and Telecom Italia Mobile (TIM).

Time zone

Italy is on Central European Time, 1 hour ahead of GMT. This means that if it is noon in Italy, it will be 11am in London and 6am in New York.

Tipping

Some restaurants in Florence levy a *coperto* or cover charge so tipping is not expected unless you patronise very expensive hotels and restaurants. If you want to give a tip, leave the small change in a bar, leave 10–15 percent in a restaurant, and round up the taxi fare.

Toilets

Public toilets are few and far between and not always clean and well maintained. All bars have toilet facilities, although visitors should at least buy a drink out of courtesy if they want to use them.

Tourist information

The Agenzia per il Turismo di Firenze (www.firenzeturismo.it) is Florence's efficient tourist information organisation. The most central office is Via Cavour 1r (tel: 055-290 832; Mon–Fri

Waiting for the tram

9am–1pm). Other offices are at the Peretola airport, Piazza San Giovanni 1 and Piazza Stazione 5.

In the UK, contact the Italian State Tourist Office (ENIT), located at 1 Princes Street, London W1B 2AY (tel: 020-7408 1254; www.enit.it).

In the US the Italian State Tourist Office is at 686 Park Avenue, New York, NY 10065 (tel: 212-586 9249; www.enit.it).

Transport

The two main airports that serve Tuscany are Florence and Pisa. Florence's small **Peretola Airport** (also known as Amerigo Vespucci; www.aeroporto.firenze.it), is about 4km (2 miles) northwest of the city centre. From London currently the direct flights are on British Airways (www.britishairways.com) and Vueling Airlines (www.vueling.com).

For most visitors flights to Pisa's **Galileo Galilei Airport** (www.pisa-airport.com), located 95km (59 miles) west of Florence, are the better option, being more frequent and usually cheaper than flights to Peretola. British Airways (www.britishairways.com), Easyjet (www.easyjet.com), Ryanair (www.ryanair.com) and Jet2 (www.jet2.com) all fly here from the UK.

There are no direct flights from US to Pisa. The best routes are via London, Brussels, Paris or Frankfurt; or to fly direct to Milan or Rome; the excellent airport train linking Rome's Fiumicino Airport with Termini station (in central Rome) and frequent, fast trains to Florence make this a good option for visitors from the US.

Arrival

Florence's Peretola Airport is connected to the city centre every 30 minutes by the Ataf-Sita (www.ataf.net) VolaInBus airport shuttle to Santa Maria Novella railway station. The journey time is about 20 minutes, and tickets are available on the bus. A taxi into the centre of Florence will cost around €20–25 and takes approximately 15 minutes. There is also a tram connection from the terminal to the city center (Piazza dell'Unità is the last stop).

From Pisa airport the simplest option is to take the Airport Bus Express by Autostradale (www.airportbusexpress.it) or the Sky Blue Lines Carolla (www.caronnatour.com) shuttle. Both of them stop near Santa Maria Novella station. The journey time is 70 minutes. Alternatively you can take a train from Pisa airport station to Florence, or the more regular train service (www.trenitalia.it) which links Florence to Pisa Centrale station, rapidly reached from the airport by train, bus or taxi. Allow 70–80 minutes for the whole journey.

By rail

The train journey from London to Florence takes around 13–18 hours via Paris and Turin or Milan. For international rail information contact Rail Europe (www.raileurope-world.com).

Public transport

The centre of Florence is small enough to cover on foot and given the heart of the city is now banned to traffic, buses included, this is the easiest way to see the city. However if you want to cross the town by public transport or visit peripheral sights there are fast and efficient electric buses (C1, C2, C3 and D) stopping near the main sights.

The local bus network, which also provides an efficient service out to suburbs such as Fiesole, is ATAF (Piazza Stazione, www.ataf.net). Tickets can be bought from tobacconists *(tabacchi)*, newsstands, bars, and from ATAF offices or automatic ticket machines at main points throughout the city, including the main transport hub of Santa Maria Novella station. You can purchase a ticket on board the bus but it will cost a good deal more. With the 90-minute ticket (€1.50) you can make as many journeys as you like. All tickets must be stamped in the appropriate machines on board the bus at the beginning of the first journey.

Line 1 of the controversial Tramvia network was opened in 2010, linking Santa Maria Novella to the suburb of Scandicci in the southwest of the city, a route rarely taken by tourists. Line 2, opened in 2019, connects Santa Maria Novella Central station and Peretola (Florence) Airport. The third line, if it ever materialises, will run from Careggi to Bagno a Ripoli.

Taxis

Taxis are white, and are hired from ranks in the main squares and at the station. They seldom stop if you hail them in the street. Taxis have meters and are also required to display fares on tariff cards. The radio taxi system is fast and efficient (tel: 055-4390 or 4242).

Driving and car hire

Florence has a city-centre driving ban and cars must be left in the car parks on the edge of the centre (www.fipark.com). You can rent cars from major companies (Hertz, Avis, Europcar, etc). Traffic travels on the right-hand side of the road, and seat belts are compulsory. Note that ALT is a stop line painted on the road at junctions; STOP is for a pedestrian crossing.

Do not leave your car on a space next to a *passo carrabile* or a *sosta vietato* sign or in a disabled space (marked in yellow).

Bicycle hire

Vehicles have been banned from the city centre in an effort to reduce congestion and pollution. Cycling is becoming increasingly popular among Florentines and there are a growing number of bike lanes. However, cyclists need their wits about them to steer a course through the hordes of tourists around the Duomo. Bicycles can be hired from Flor-

Glorious views over the Tuscan hills

ence By Bike, Via San Zanobi 54r, tel: 055-488 992, www.florencebybike.it or Alinari, Via San Zanobi 38r, tel: 055-280 500, www.alinarirental.com. Florence Town (www.florencetown.com) offer 2.5-hour guided 'I Bike Florence' tours, from March to October daily at 10am and 3pm (from May to September also at 6pm).

Visas and passports

Citizens from EU countries require a passport or a Visitor's Identification Card to enter Italy. A visa is not required. Holders of passports from most other countries do not require visas for stays of fewer than three months, except for nationals of some Eastern European countries, who need to obtain visas from the Italian Embassy in their own country. After Brexit, UK travellers will not need a visa to visit Italy if the stay is no longer than 90 days every six months.

Youth hostels

Contact your national youth hostel association before departure to obtain an international membership card. Hostelling International (www.hihostels. com) has one hostel in the area, in a converted villa on the outskirts of Florence, a 30 minute bus trip from the centre in Fiesole: Ostello Villa Camerata (Viale A. Righi 4; tel: 055-532 6194). In the Tuscan countryside 30km (19 miles) from Florence is the Ostello del Chianti (Via Roma 137, Tavernelle Val di Pesa; tel: 055-805 0265).

There are several other hostels in Florence, some more centrally located than the Hostelling International one. Ostello Santa Monaca (Via Santa Monaca 6, tel: 055-268 338, www.ostellosantamonaca.com) is in a 16th century convent not far from Santa Maria Novella Central Station. The more recent Plus Florence Hostel (Via Santa Caterina d'Alessandria 15, tel: 055-628 6347, www.humancompany.com), complete with swimming pool, bar, terrace and flat-screen TVs, is located northeast of the station.

Weights and measures

The metric system is used for weights and measures. Italians refer to 100 grams as *un etto*; 200 grams are therefore *due etti* and so on.

Women travellers

The difficulties encountered by women travelling in Italy are overstated. However, women do, especially if they are young and blonde, have to put up with male attention. Ignoring whistles and questions is the best way to get rid of unwanted attention. The less you look like a tourist, the fewer problems you will have.

Bilingual safety sign

LANGUAGE

Most hotels have staff who speak some English, and unless you go well off the beaten track, you should have little problem communicating in shops or restaurants. However, there are places not on the tourist circuit where you will have the chance to practise your Italian, and local people will think more of you for making an effort. It is well worth buying a good phrase book or dictionary, but here are a few basics to help you get started.

Useful phrases

Yes *Sì*
No *No*
Thank you *Grazie*
Many thanks *Mille grazie/Tante grazie*
You're welcome *Prego*
All right/That's fine *Va bene*
Please *Per favore/Per cortesia*
Excuse me (to get attention) *Scusi*
Excuse me (in a crowd) *Permesso*
Certainly *Ma, certo/Certamente*
Can you show me...? *Può indicarmi...?*
Can you help me, please? *Può aiutarmi, per cortesia?*
I need... *Ho bisogno di...*
I'm lost *Mi sono perso*
I'm sorry *Mi dispiace*
I don't know *Non lo so*
I don't understand *Non capisco*
Do you speak English/French/Spanish? *Parla inglese/francese/spagnolo?*
Could you speak more slowly? *Può parlare più lentamente, per favore?*

Could you repeat that please? *Può ripetere, per piacere?*
How much does it cost? *quanto costa?*
this one/that one *questo/quello*
Have you got...? *Avete...?*

At a bar/restaurant
I'd like to book a table *Vorrei prenotare un tavolo*
Have you got a table for... *Avete un tavolo per...*
I have a reservation *Ho prenotato*
lunch/supper *il pranzo/la cena*
I'm a vegetarian *Sono vegetariano/a*
What would you like? *Che cosa prende?*
I'd like... *Vorrei...*
mineral water fizzy/still *acqua minerale gasata/naturale*
a bottle of *una bottiglia di*
a glass of *un bicchieri di*
red/white wine *vino rosso/bianco*
beer *una birra*
milk *latte*
sandwich/roll *un tramezzino/un panino*
the dish of the day *il piatto del giorno*

On the menu
antipasto misto **mixed hors d'oeuvres: cold cuts, cheeses, roast vegetables (ask for details)**
antipasto di verdura **vegetable**
antipasto di pesce **fish**
arrosto **roast**
al forno **baked**
alla griglia **grilled**

Do try and speak a little Italian

il maiale **pork**
il manzo **beef**
il pollo **chicken**
affumicato **smoked**
alla griglia **grilled**
fritto **fried**
il pesce **fish**
le vongole **clams**
i crostacei **shellfish**
i contorni **side dishes**
insalata caprese **fresh tomato, basil and mozzarella salad**

Getting around

What time do you open/close? *A che ora apre/chiude?*
Closed for the holidays (typical sign) *Chiuso per ferie*
ferry terminal *la stazione marittima*
Where can I buy tickets? *Dove posso fare i biglietti?*
What time does the train/ferry leave? *A che ora parte il treno/vaporetto?*
Can you tell me where to get off? *Mi può dire dove devo scendere?*
right/left *a destra/a sinistra*
Go straight on *Va sempre diritto*

Online

Where's an internet cafe? *Dov'è un Internet caffè?*
Does it have wireless internet? *C'è il wireless?*
What is the Wi-Fi password? *Qual è la password Wi-Fi?*
Is the Wi-Fi free? *Il WiFi è gratis?*
Do you have bluetooth? *Avete il Bluetooth*

How do I turn the computer on/off? *Come si accende/spegne il computer?*
Can I…? *Posso…?*
access the internet *collegarmi (a Internet)*
check e-mail *controllare le e-mail*
print *stampare*
plug in/charge my laptop/iPhone/iPad/BlackBerry? *collegare/ricaricare il mio portatile/iPhone/iPad?*
access Skype? *usare Skype?*
How much per hour/half hour? *Quanto costa per un'ora/mezz'ora?*
How do I…? *Come…?*
connect/disconnect *ci si collega/scollega*
log on/log off *si fa il login/logout*
What's your e-mail? *Qual è la sua e-mail?*
My e-mail is… *La mia e-mail è…*
Do you have a scanner? *Avete uno scanner?*

Social media

Are you on Facebook/Twitter? *È su Facebook/Twitter?*
What's your user name? *Qual è il suo nome utente?*
I'll add you as a friend. *La aggiungerò come amico.*
I'll follow you on Twitter. *La seguirò su Twitter.*
Are you following…? *Segue…?*
I'll put the pictures on Facebook/Twitter. *Metterò le foto su Facebook/Twitter.*
I'll tag you in the pictures. *La taggherò nelle foto.*

BOOKS AND FILM

Books

Art and architecture

The Architecture of the Italian Renaissance. Peter Murray. Originally published in 1967, this volume by a professor of Birkbeck College, London, remains the classic guide to art and architecture of the Renaissance period.

Autobiography. Benvenuto Cellini. The troubled life of the Florentine artist gives an insight into life in the Renaissance period.

Brunelleschi's Dome: The Story of a Great Cathedral in Florence. This book charts one of the greatest architectural feats ever to have been accomplished – the dome of Santa Maria del Fiore cathedral – and its creator.

Florence: The City & Its Architecture. Richard Goy. Organised thematically as opposed to chronologically, this is a modern account of the history, culture, politics and art of Florence. Includes drawings and photographs.

The Florentine Renaissance. Vincent Cronin. A comprehensive guide to the years of the Renaissance and its intellectual output.

Italian Architecture from Michelangelo to Borromini. Antony Hopkins. Tracking the artistic period from the High Renaissance through Mannerism to Baroque, this helps explain the background to much of Florence's artistic patrimony.

Lives of the Artists: Volumes 1 and 2. Giorgio Vasari . An account of the lives of many important figures in Florentine art by the figure renowned for the corridor linking the Palazzo Vecchio to Palazzo Pitti via the Uffizi.

Villas of Tuscany. Carlo Cresti & Massimo Listri. Writing and photographs about Tuscan houses, including the Medici villas around Florence, designed by masters such as Buontalenti.

Culture and history

The City of Florence: Historical Vistas and Personal Sightings. R.W.B. Lewis. A personal view on Florence and its legacy – the perfect travel companion.

Dark Water: Art, Disaster and Redemption in Florence. Robert Clark. Gripping description of the floods which ravaged Florence in 1966 – and the aftermath.

Florence: The Biography of a City. Christopher Hibbert. This book weaves together the history and culture of Florence, with photographs and illustrations to make the narrative come to life.

The Rise and Fall of the House of Medici. Christopher Hibbert. By an author who has written extensively on Florence, this book provides a witty insight into the dynasty which ruled Florence and is responsible for gathering much of the art to be found there today.

Tuscany and Its Wines. Hugh Johnson and Andy Katz. Providing a guide to the best wines in the region, with stunning pictures by photographer Andy Katz.

Literature

A Room with a View. E.M. Forster. Forster's classic novel and social study of class and the mores of the English holidaying in Florence in the Edwardian period.

Love and War in the Apennines. Eric Newby. A story of the escape of a British prisoner of war in Italy in World War II.

The Prince. Niccolò Machiavelli. Machiavelli's classic treatise on power in the Renaissance.

A Traveller's Companion to Florence. Harold Acton and Edward Chaney, Eds. An overview of Florence, based on letters and memoirs from several renowned Florentine ex-pat personalities.

The Da Vinci Code. Dan Brown. This best-selling thriller is based in Western history and includes interesting titbits relevant to Italy and Florence.

D.H. Lawrence and Italy. D.H. Lawrence. Three books based on Lawrence's journals during his travels in Italy which make an interesting travel companion.

The Enchantress of Florence. Salmon Rushdie. A rich blend of history, folly and fantasy where East (Mogul India) meets West (Renaissance Florence).

Florence Explored. Rupert Scott. A great little book, which is presented through a series of walks around the city.

Italian Hours. Henry James. Essays on 19th-century travel in Italy by another classic author.

Pictures from Italy. Charles Dickens. A travelogue of Dickens's tour of Italy, which he took during a break from writing.

War in the Val d'Orcia. Iris Origo. A true story of civilian life in Tuscany during World War II.

Under the Tuscan Sun. Frances Mayes. This and two later books, Bella Tuscany and Every Day in Tuscany, tell the story of an American who has chosen Tuscany as her new home.

Films

A Room with a View (1985). An acclaimed adaptation of the novel by E.M. Forster starring Maggie Smith, Helena Bonham-Carter and Simon Callow.

Tea with Mussolini (1999). Starring Judi Dench and Maggie Smith, the film charts the life of a boy left in the care of a millionairess and three eccentric British women in Florence during the Fascist occupation of Italy.

Under the Tuscan Sun (2003). The story of a woman in search of a new life in Tuscany.

Certified Copy (2010). A Tuscan antique shop owner and a British writer are mistakenly taken as husband and wife. Starring Juliette Binoche.

Italian cinema has also produced some classic films (*Cinema Paradiso*, *La Dolce Vita*, *La Vita è Bella*), actors and actresses (Sophia Loren, Monica Bellucci) and directors (Franco Zeffirelli, Federico Fellini). The most famous films can be found subtitled.

ABOUT THIS BOOK

This *Explore Guide* has been produced by the editors of Insight Guides, whose books have set the standard for visual travel guides since 1970. With top-quality photography and authoritative recommendations, these guidebooks bring you the very best routes and itineraries in the world's most exciting destinations.

BEST ROUTES

The routes in the book provide something to suit all budgets, tastes and trip lengths. As well as covering the destination's many classic attractions, the itineraries track lesser-known sights, and there are also excursions for those who want to extend their visit outside the city. The routes embrace a range of interests, so whether you are an art fan, a gourmet, a history buff or have kids to entertain, you will find an option to suit.

We recommend reading the whole of a route before setting out. This should help you to familiarise yourself with it and enable you to plan where to stop for refreshments – options are shown in the 'Food and Drink' box at the end of each tour.

For our pick of the tours by theme, consult Recommended Routes for… (see pages 6–7).

INTRODUCTION

The routes are set in context by this introductory section, giving an overview of the destination to set the scene, plus background information on food and drink, shopping and more, while a succinct history timeline highlights the key events over the centuries.

DIRECTORY

Also supporting the routes is a Directory chapter, with a clearly organised A–Z of practical information, our pick of where to stay while you are there and select restaurant listings; these eateries complement the more low-key cafés and restaurants that feature within the routes and are intended to offer a wider choice for evening dining. Also included here are some nightlife listings, plus a handy language guide and our recommendations for books and films about the destination.

ABOUT THE AUTHORS

Susie Boulton is a travel writer and art historian who has been a regular visitor to Florence for some 30 years. She first fell in love with Florence and Tuscany as a student, selling ice creams to pay for accommodation. She is the author of a dozen guides to Italy. Other contributors include Hilary Weston and Jackie Staddon.

CONTACT THE EDITORS

We hope you find this Explore Guide useful, interesting and a pleasure to read. If you have any questions or feedback on the text, pictures or maps, please do let us know. If you have noticed any errors or outdated facts, or have suggestions for places to include on the routes, we would be delighted to hear from you. Please drop us an email at hello@insightguides.com. Thanks!

CREDITS

Explore Florence
Editor: Sian Marsh
Author: Susie Boulton
Head of DTP and Pre-Press: Rebeka Davies
Update Production: Apa Digital
Managing Editor: Carine Tracanelli
Picture Editor: Tom Smyth
Cartography: original cartography Berndston & Berndston, updated by Carte
Photo credits: Alamy 136, 137; Antonio Quattrone/Museo dell'Opera del Duomo 35; AWL Images 1, 26/27T; Belomond 109; Britta Jaschinski/Apa Publications 4ML, 4MC, 4MR, 4ML, 6MC, 6ML, 7MR, 8MC, 8ML, 10T, 10B, 11L, 10/11, 12B, 12/13, 16, 16/17T, 17T, 17M, 18T, 18B, 19, 20, 20/21T, 21T, 21M, 26ML, 28, 30, 30/31, 31L, 32T, 32B, 34, 36, 36/37, 37L, 38T, 38B, 38/39, 39L, 40, 41, 45, 48, 49L, 48/49, 52, 53L, 54, 55, 56, 58, 59, 60, 60/61, 61L, 62, 63, 64, 65, 67, 68, 69, 70, 71, 72, 73, 74, 75, 77, 78, 80, 81, 82, 83, 110, 110/111, 111L, 112, 113, 116, 116/117, 117L, 121, 123, 124, 125, 126, 128, 129, 132, 133; Corbis 14B, 23T, 66, 86, 120; Fotolia 4MC, 4/5T, 6BC, 8MR, 8/9T, 84, 87, 100/101T; Getty Images 24, 25T; iStock 6TL, 7M, 22, 23B, 44, 94, 95, 96, 97, 98/99; Leonardo 104, 105, 106, 107, 108; Mockford & Bonetti/Apa Publications 8ML, 8MC, 12T, 13L, 29, 33, 50, 51, 52/53, 57, 79, 127; Rocco Forte Hotels 114, 115; Royal Demeure Hotles 102, 102/103, 103L; Scala Archives 46, 47, 85; Shutterstock 25B; Starwood Hotles & Resorts 100ML; Steve McDonald/Apa Publications 4MR, 7T, 7MR, 8MR, 14/15T, 26MC, 26MR, 26ML, 26MC, 26MR, 42, 43, 88, 89, 90, 91, 92, 92/93, 93L, 100MC, 100MR, 100MR, 100MC, 100ML, 118, 119, 122, 130/131, 134, 135; Tom Smyth 76
Cover credits: Pietro Canali/4Corners Images (main) iStock (bottom)

Printed by CTPS – China

DISTRIBUTION

UK, Ireland and Europe
Apa Publications (UK) Ltd
sales@insightguides.com
United States and Canada
Ingram Publisher Services
ips@ingramcontent.com
Australia and New Zealand
Woodslane
info@woodslane.com.au
Southeast Asia
Apa Publications (Singapore) Pte
singaporeoffice@insightguides.com
Worldwide
Apa Publications (UK) Ltd
sales@insightguides.com

SPECIAL SALES, CONTENT LICENSING AND COPUBLISHING

Insight Guides can be purchased in bulk quantities at discounted prices. We can create special editions, personalised jackets and corporate imprints tailored to your needs.
sales@insightguides.com
www.insightguides.biz

INDEX

MAP LEGEND

● Start of tour

— Tour & route direction

❶ Recommended sight

❷ Recommended
    restaurant/café

★ Place of interest

❶ Tourist information

🛉 Statue/monument

✉ Main post office

🚌 Main bus station

▢ Park

▢ Important building

▢ Hotel

▢ Transport hub

▢ Shop / market

▢ Pedestrian area

▢ Urban area

INSIGHT ⊙ GUIDES

OFF THE SHELF

Since 1970, INSIGHT GUIDES has provided a unique perspective on the world's best travel destinations by using specially commissioned photography and illuminating text written by local authors.

Whether you're planning a city break, a walking tour or the journey of a lifetime, our superb range of guidebooks and phrasebooks will inspire you to discover more about your chosen destination.

INSIGHT GUIDES

offer a unique combination of stunning photos, absorbing narrative and detailed maps, providing all the inspiration and information you need.

PHRASEBOOKS & DICTIONARIES

help users to feel at home, when away. Pocket-sized with a free app to download, they go where you do.

CITY GUIDES

pack hundreds of great photos into a smaller format with detailed practical information, so you can navigate the world's top cities with confidence.

EXPLORE GUIDES

feature easy-to-follow walks and itineraries in the world's most exciting destinations, with our choice of the best places to eat and drink along the way.

POCKET GUIDES

combine concise information on where to go and what to do in a handy compact format, ideal on the ground. Includes a full-colour, fold-out map.

EXPERIENCE GUIDES

feature offbeat perspectives and secret gems for experienced travellers, with a collection of over 100 ideas for a memorable stay in a city.

www.insightguides.com